2—

BEAUTIFUL ZION

Impressions of Church History

All artwork copyright © by Al Rounds. For print information go to www.alrounds.com.
Text copyright © 2008 by S. Michael Wilcox
Jacket and book design by Jessica A. Warner, © 2008 Covenant Communications, Inc.

Published by Covenant Communications, Inc.
American Fork, Utah

Printed in China
First Printing: October 2008

15 14 13 12 11 10 09 08   10 9 8 7 6 5 4 3 2 1

ISBN-13 978-1-59811-594-9
ISBN-10 1-59811-594-4

Art by *Al Rounds*   Text by *S. Michael Wilcox*

BEAUTIFUL ZION

Impressions of Church History

INTRODUCTION

WHEN I WAS A BOY, I dreamed of visiting faraway places where mighty things had been done by great people. Train whistles called hauntingly to me with promises of vast distances ending at the high points of historical legacy or natural wonders of creation. Those marvels called to me not only because of their beauty, but because they were forged in the deep epochs of earlier ages. They were older than man!

I would sometimes stand on the railroad tracks and stare down their narrowing gauge until they merged at a vanishing point. They seemed to fade not only into space, but into time. Then the old familiar tug of the past would pull at my heart and a longing would rise up and take me into the world of daydream. I have felt a restlessness all my life, one too strong to inherit only a small portion of the earth or its passage through time. I have envied the wind.

Midway View of Timpanogos

With its span of open fields, mature trees, working irrigation ditches, and barbed-wire fences (designed mostly to keep out wandering livestock), the Midway Valley—and valleys like it—often become my models for my historical paintings. The backdrop of snow-capped mountains and the quiet rural atmosphere engender in me a great feeling for what the Salt Lake Valley used to look like.

Since those first stirrings of my youth, I have found the hunger enlarged as my knowledge grew. Yet, in His infinite mercy, God has fulfilled more than I ever could have hoped. I have walked the fields of my childhood daydreams and known the memory and the wisdom of the land; I have sensed the people who blessed it and who changed the times. None has been more significant and poignant than those connected with the Prophet Joseph Smith—those he touched and those who followed him.

I have found fellow travelers on the paths of the past who shared this longing to encompass time's endless dimensions and the earth's stretching circumference. I remember standing on the battlefield of Gettysburg a number of years ago and being overwhelmed by the words of one of its most famous heroes, for I knew I had found a kindred spirit.

"In great deeds something abides," Joshua Lawrence Chamberlain wrote. "On great fields something stays. Forms change and pass; bodies disappear; but spirits linger, to consecrate ground for the vision place of souls. And reverent men and women from afar, and generations that know us not and that we know not of, heart-drawn to see where and by whom great

> *Forms change and pass; bodies disappear; but spirits linger, to consecrate ground for the vision place of souls.*

things were suffered and done for them, shall come to this deathless field, to ponder and dream; and lo! The shadow of a mighty presence shall wrap them in its bosom and the power of vision pass into their souls."

Since I first saw Al Rounds' paintings, I knew he too had felt the sweet ache and yearning for the past. I have four of them hanging on my walls. He has honored me in asking if I would write the text to accompany much of his life's work. It has captured and holds the "mighty presence" of our shared Restoration legacy and it will bring one as close to the consecrated ground, the actual "vision place of souls," as one can achieve—just short of standing there in reality while the land's memory draws you back through the intervening years. We hope the journey we take you on through the pages of this publication will stir your own passion for the past and increase our shared faith and gratitude for a story of sacrifice and joy. May those spirits who linger stay a little, and wrap us in the comforting mantles of the past, that we may share their power of vision.

New York Period

SACRED GROVE

Sacred Grove, Winter

Winter with its simplicity has always been my favorite time of year. For farmers, the pace slows considerably—and winter would have given Joseph Smith hours of uninterrupted time, not only near the grove but in his home, to ponder on the magnificent things he had received from the Lord.

IT ALL BEGAN IN A GROVE of trees, and in the simplest of ways—a boy prayed. This is God's way. All the light and the glory would follow—golden plates with tales of iron rods and titles of liberty, resurrected ancient prophets sharing priesthood keys, the promised perfection of Zion, living Apostles speaking wisdom in yearly conferences, bishops, wards, stakes, universities, a choir, patriarchs, pioneers and Primary, a women's organization, handcarts, white-shirted missionaries, tabernacles and temples, baptisms for the dead, endowment, celestial marriage—Godhood. It is the great pageant of "the fulness of times," when all the most precious inheritances of past civilizations would be coupled with things never before revealed to man, truths "which have been kept hid from before the foundation of the world" (D&C 124:41). Joseph's words, "Father in Heaven . . . ," pierced the veil, and from its separated curtains flowed

personal writings of *Joseph Smith*

I cried unto the Lord for mercy for there was none else to whom I could go and obtain mercy and the Lord heard my cry in the wilderness.

. . . I was filled with the spirit of god and the Lord opened the heavens upon me and I saw the Lord and he spake unto me saying Joseph, my son, thy sins are forgiven thee. . . . and my soul was filled with love and for many days I could rejoice with great Joy and the Lord was with me . . .

(*Personal Writings of Joseph Smith,* comp. Dean Jesse [Salt Lake City: Deseret Book, 1984], 11–12.)

the pent-up energy of Godly gifts held back through the centuries by the darkness of ignorance and fear.

I remember visiting the Sacred Grove one year "on the morning of a beautiful, clear day, early in the spring" (JS–H 1:14). I anticipated I would enter a "shady woodland" alive with the sound of "bees… humming" and "sweet birds singing, music ringing thru the grove" (*Hymns,* No. 26). But New York in the early spring presents a different picture than the one I had imagined through so many singings of "Joseph Smith's First Prayer." The trees were fresh with buds, the ground still moist from renewing rains and melting snow. The quiet spaces between the trees spoke with a different sound, the reverence of Beginnings.

In 1820 it was more than the opening of a new year, but of a new dispensation, a new revelation binding the heavens with the earth, uniting the Father with His fourteen-year-old son and that son with the Father's "Beloved" One. Here is the great symbol of the Restoration, the moment of possibilities for us all, portrayed by a kneeling boy immersed in a "pillar of light" (JS–H 1:16).

The Grove was empty when I entered it, and I was alone with my thoughts. Yet the memories of the land walked with me while the familiar phrases lingered through my musings, and the message of that "first" morning's vision became as clear as the cool spring air. I was struck again by the profound humility of Joseph's own description as he looked back eighteen years to his fourteen-year-old self. "I was an obscure boy . . . " he wrote, "a boy of no consequence in the world . . . " (JS–H 1:22). Yet, surely, only one other boy, also raised in obscure circumstances—the carpenter's shop of Nazareth—was of greater consequence than Joseph Smith. We are all obscure boys and girls of no consequence in the world, but if God spoke to Joseph, then He will speak to us also. Indeed, this is the theme of Joseph's life, the reason God sent him to us.

Joseph Smith addressed his testimony to "all inquirers after truth." Herein is our challenge and the challenge Joseph laid before the world. Is it truth we seek or our "own tenets"; the "commandments of men," which have ever created a "war of words and tumult of opinions," or "wisdom from God"? Yet opinions of truth always lack redemptive grace, and Joseph was not content to merely "file off, some to one

If God spoke to Joseph, then He will speak to us also.

party and some to another." No, he wanted a "certain conclusion," wanted to know "how to act," wanted "wisdom from God," wanted "confidence in settling the question." He was the quintessential inquirer after truth, the supreme example of all we must strive to be if we would find certain conclusions and settled questions concerning the will of God or the private dilemmas of our own lives. (See JS–H 1:6-12.)

And more! The Father and the Son knew this boy would act on the answers he would receive—not only those acknowledged in the new spring growth of Palmyra, but those of Fayette, Harmony, Kirtland, Hiram, Independence, Liberty, Far West, and Nauvoo. This inquirer after truth would give the world a whole book of settled questions—the Doctrine and Covenants. He continued seeking wisdom from God until the gunfire of Carthage silenced his insatiable hunger for truth.

I thought of the persecutions that "would fill up volumes," persecutions Joseph said "arose against me, almost in my infancy," but he "continued to affirm" and "assert" he had seen a vision. Act! Affirm! Assert! The words ring like the tolling bells of a renewed Christendom, breaking the quiet of the trees and the winter chill of ages of silent apostasy where boys knew not that they could pray and hear the voice of God. (See JS–H 1:20, 27, 58, 61.)

As I left the Grove that morning I knew why God had chosen this particular obscure boy, this "disturber and annoyer of [Satan's] kingdom." He knew Joseph Smith was a true inquirer after truth, one who wanted certain conclusions and settled questions, and would act, affirm, and assert the answers he received "and all the world could not make him think or believe otherwise." This is what he was sent to teach us! This is what we each must do when we enter our own sacred groves seeking pillars of light. (See JS–H 1:20, 24.)

I called on the Lord in mighty prayer, a pillar of fire appeared above my head, it presently rested down upon me, and filled me with Joy unspeakable . . .

(*Personal Writings of Joseph Smith,* comp. Dean Jesse [Salt Lake City: Deseret Book, 1984], 105.)

Sacred Grove

I spent quite a bit of time in the Sacred Grove at about the same time of year as Joseph went there to utter his humble prayer. During the first week of April in upstate New York, there are no leaves on the trees—they are just beginning to bud. What Joseph describes as a beautiful spring morning says a lot about his disposition: in reality, the trees were bare, the ground was covered with debris, and it was very likely wet and cold. But Joseph saw light and felt warmth—not from the things in nature, but from He who created nature . . . and it was, indeed, beautiful.

LOG HOME

After Much Contemplation

This painting comes from a dream I had as a young man; Joseph stood in front of the Smith cabin—a structure I didn't know at the time even existed—and it was clear to me that he had just experienced the First Vision. He stood with a wooden pitchfork in his hand. As an impressionable boy of fourteen, he must have thought that all would now change, but it didn't—his father still thrust the pitchfork into his hand and asked that he shovel manure from the barn. Yet there would come incredible changes, and Joseph knew it. . . .

IN SPITE OF THE WARMING POWER of the First Vision, the joy and the love it produced within him, Joseph Smith was completely human. "Mingling with all kinds of society," he wrote, "I frequently fell into many foolish errors, and displayed the weakness of youth, and the foibles of human nature; which, I am sorry to say, led me into divers temptations, offensive in the sight of God. . . . In consequence of these things, I often felt condemned for my weakness and imperfections . . . " (JS–H 1:28–29). How often have I felt a kinship to these words and gratitude that Joseph was a man with whom I share frail humanity. Later in his life, he wrote: "The nearer we get to our heavenly Father, the more we are disposed to look with compassion on perishing souls; we feel that we want to take them upon our shoulders, and cast their sins behind our backs" (Joseph Fielding Smith, *Teachings of the Prophet Joseph Smith* [Salt Lake City: Deseret Book, 1938], 241).

This was a tipping point in God's dealing in the affairs of men, a fulcrum of spiritual history.

In the humility of failed perfection, Joseph sought his Father. "I betook myself to prayer . . . for forgiveness . . ." (JS–H 1:29). And God responded. In the upstairs room of the log home, Moroni came with a vision of Cumorah and plates that captured in their golden glow wondrous stories of ocean voyages, stripling warriors, and the Savior at Bountiful blessing each child "one by one" (3 Nephi 17:21).

To this boy "guilty of levity" and "associated with jovial company," Moroni unfolded the majestic dimensions of his call. He turned his eyes to the distant future. The angel told Joseph that "God had a work for me to do; and that my name should be had for good and evil among all nations, kindreds, and tongues. . . ." In the decades and centuries to come Joseph would be known and reverenced in the streets of London, Frankfurt, Moscow, Tokyo, Sao Paolo, and Sydney, as he is today, and will yet be in Beijing, Cairo, Havana, and Islamabad. (See JS–H 1:28, 33.)

Then, from the future, Moroni turned Joseph's eyes through the mists of the past to ancient prophets who saw his day and recorded its wonders. Isaiah, Malachi, Joel, and Peter sensed with a seer's insight the work he would be entrusted with. This thing would also not be "done in a corner" (Acts 26:26). It was a tipping point in God's dealing in the affairs of men, a fulcrum of spiritual history, a hinge whose arch traced the boundaries of many millenniums. His work was to be played out on a vast continuum of time undoubtedly incomprehensible to the teenaged farm boy, but so apparent now. So, Joseph had much to learn, and his education was soon to become intense at Moroni's school room—the hill that came to be called Cumorah.

Prophets of Old
prophesied of Joseph's work

MALACHI: Behold, I will reveal unto you the Priesthood, by the hand of Elijah the prophet . . .

ISAIAH: And there shall come forth a rod out of the stem of Jesse, and a Branch shall grow out of his roots: And the spirit of the Lord shall rest upon him, the spirit of wisdom and understanding, the spirit of counsel and might, the spirit of knowledge and of the fear of the Lord; And shall make him of quick understanding in the fear of the Lord: and he shall not judge after the sight of his eyes, neither reprove after the hearing of his ears: But with righteousness shall he judge . . . and reprove . . .

JOEL: And it shall come to pass afterward, that I will pour out my spirit upon all flesh; and your sons and your daughters shall prophesy, your old men shall dream dreams, your young men shall see visions:

(See JS–H 36–41.)

HILL CUMORAH

THE HILL CUMORAH IS NOT VERY LARGE, but I never climb to its summit without a sense that I am entering into the once very intimate and private domain of two prophets—one ancient, one modern—who shared many wondrous conversations in its cloaked forest seclusion. Here Moroni shaped and molded the boy into the man. The last solitary wanderer of a ruined society, unheeded in his own life, now had a pupil with a mind that could penetrate the deepest mysteries of eternity.

Joseph spoke of the "weakness of youth" as it was displayed in his own life. I have often pondered that phrase, wondering if it contained insight that could strengthen youth in every generation. Joseph would face a temptation when he first arrived at the Hill Cumorah. Moroni cautioned him, telling him, "Satan would try to tempt me (in consequence of the indigent circumstances of my father's family), to get the plates for the purpose of getting rich." But the plates were to "glorify God" and for that purpose alone. No "other motive" must influence the seventeen-year-old boy. With the assurance that God the Father and the Son were realities and aware of him; with four intense instructional sessions with Moroni immediately alive in his memory; with his natural good character ("a disposition to commit . . . [malignant sins] . . . was

The record was found . . . on the west side of the hill, not far from the top down its side; and when myself visited the place in the year 1830, there were several trees standing: . . .

(Oliver Cowdery, *Messenger and Advocate*, Letter 8, 2:196, Oct. 1835.)

___ Hill Cumorah

The view looking back from the Hill Cumorah towards the Manchester farm of Joseph Smith's family and the Sacred Grove.

never in my nature"); with Moroni's planted sense of the time-spanning wonder and nature of his call weighing "deep…on my mind"; with the encouragement and believing support of his father; and with the specific warning of Moroni regarding the very temptation that awaited him—Joseph stepped into the road from the Smith farm to the Hill Cumorah. (See JS–H 1:28, 46.)

He could have walked the two to three miles in roughly an hour to an hour and a half. What turmoil rolled through his young mind as he covered that distance? With what anticipation did he climb the hill, find the envisioned stone, and, using a lever, roll it off its almost fifteen-hundred-year resting place? Oliver Cowdery gives us a glimpse into Joseph's thoughts.

"Alternately . . . the thought of the previous vision was ruminating in his mind, with a reflection of the brightness and glory of the heavenly messenger; but again a thought would start across the mind on the prospects of obtaining so desirable a treasure. . . . Here was a struggle indeed; for when he calmly reflected upon his errand, he knew that if God did not give, he could not obtain; and again, with the thought or hope of obtaining, his mind would be carried

back to its former reflection of poverty, abuse, wealth, grandeur and ease, until before arriving at the place described, this wholly occupied his desire" ("Truth Will Prevail," *Times and Seasons* 2:12, April 15, 1841, 364–377).

Joseph made three attempts to remove the record but received a shock that drained him of strength, each time of increasing force. "Why can I not obtain this book?" he cried. "Because you have not kept the commandments of the Lord," answered Moroni. How quickly all he had been taught and shown returned, then humility replaced the lure of golden plates as a source of wealth, and he remembered. "Do not understand me to attach blame to our brother," Oliver continued, "he was young, and his mind easily turned from correct principles, unless he could be favored with a certain round of experience" (Oliver Cowdery, *Messenger and Advocate,* Letter 8, 2:197–198, Oct. 1835).

What is the "weakness of youth?" Is it not a lack of experience? Until that maturity is gained we must learn to trust the Moronis of our lives: those to whom life has granted wisdom, such as our prophets and Apostles. Joseph's education was about to begin in earnest, an education designed by his angelic tutor to give him "experience." "The heavens were opened and the glory of the Lord shone round about and rested upon him. While he thus stood gazing and admiring, the angel said, 'Look!' and as he thus spake he beheld the prince of darkness. . . . 'All this is shown the good and the evil, the holy and impure, the glory of God and the power of darkness, that you may know hereafter the two powers and never be influenced or overcome by that wicked one'" (Oliver Cowdery, *Messenger and Advocate,* Letter 8, 2:198, Oct. 1835).

His mother related that these visions were sufficient "that ever afterwards he was willing to keep the commandments of God" (Lucy Mack Smith, *History of Joseph Smith by His Mother* [Salt Lake City: Stevens and Wallis, Inc., 1945], 81). Joseph was an able learner. What wonderful, yet intense, moments Joseph must have enjoyed in those yearly sessions with Moroni as he showed him "what the Lord was going to do, and how and in what manner his kingdom was to be conducted in the last days" (JS–H 1:54).

Joseph Smith Sr. Frame Home

I painted this picture of the Joseph Smith Sr. family home in Manchester (Palmyra), New York, long before the home was restored in 2002. Alvin (Joseph's oldest brother), who had apprenticed as a builder, started construction on the home and had completed the frame by the fall of 1823, but that November Alvin died. Joseph Smith Sr. moved his family into the home late in 1825, even though it still needed finishing work. Joseph brought his new bride, Emma, to live here in January 1827. Eight months later he was allowed to retrieve the golden plates from the Hill Cumorah, and kept them hidden in and around this home until the persecution became too great and the couple moved to Harmony, Pennsylvania, to live with Emma's family. The site designated as the Sacred Grove is located just across the street.

THE LONG NIGHT'S CONVERSATIONS had weakened Joseph and, sensing he was not well, his father sent him home. Crossing a fence he lost his strength and "was quite unconscious of anything" (JS–H 1:48). Recovering, he was greeted once again by Moroni. "The first thing he said was, 'Why did you not tell your father that which I commanded you to tell him?' Joseph replied, 'I was afraid my father would not believe me.' The angel rejoined, 'He will believe every word you say to him'" (Lucy Mack Smith, 79). Joseph obeyed Moroni and immediately returned to his "father in the field and rehearsed the whole matter to him. He replied . . . that it was of God, and told me to go and do as commanded by the messenger" (JS–H 1:50).

One of the most endearing images I hold in my mind of the Prophet Joseph is that of him and his father pausing from the more mundane work of the farm

IN THE FIELD AT THE SMITH FARM

He Will Believe Every Word

This painting depicts Joseph Smith in the field telling his father of the visit and message of the angel Moroni in September 1823. Joseph was reluctant to tell his father, but at the repeated command of Moroni and encouragement of "he will believe every word," Joseph did so. His father was willing to set down the tools and the pressures of the day and listen. And he did believe. This painting means a lot to me because there is such a powerful message conveyed when someone will sit down and listen to you, feel what you feel, understand, and believe . . . especially when the pressures of the day say "this is not a good time."

Joseph Smith

speaks of his family

I will tell you what I want. If tomorrow I shall be called to lie in yonder tomb, in the morning of the resurrection let me strike hands with my father, and cry, "My father," and he will say, "My son, my son," . . . .

And when the voice calls for the dead to arise, suppose I am laid by the side of my father, what would be the first joy of my heart? To meet my father, my mother, my brother, my sister; and when they are by my side, I embrace them and they me.

(Teachings of the Prophet Joseph Smith, 295–96.)

to converse on the heavenly work of God. Did they sit on the ground in the fall furrows, or did they lean against a stoop of grain? Were the horses glad for work's reprieve, and were the silent scythes hushed from their swinging arch? There is a hallowed beauty surrounding the scene, the sacred trust of family.

We are a family church, and we hold that institution as the foundation of our faith. What a magnificent family God chose for Joseph. The first family of the Restoration is a model for us all. How complete they were in their unwavering support for their son and brother and husband. Moroni knew that family. "He will believe every word you say to him," could be said of all the Smiths, and in time it could also be said of Joseph's wife, Emma. How many similar scenes of that family could we call up to inspire our own?

We watch the Smiths from the father tenderly holding in his arms the boy with the infected leg to those last poignant seconds in Carthage with Hyrum—and a hundred in between. From New York, through Ohio and Missouri, to Illinois, in spite of difficulties and their own human weaknesses, no one faltered, no one despaired, no one doubted. Joseph had been called of God, come what may, and the end would find them true. These are the moments that bind up the eternal knots within caring and committed souls.

The first family of the Restoration is a model for us all.

I have been a reader of history for as long as I can remember, and it has always troubled me to see how readily the human race allows the spirit of persecution, brutality, intolerance, and mean-mindedness to prevail. It is so often remarkable to see how powerful religion can be in shutting down the mind from thinking and the heart from feeling. It is in the recorded memory of crusades and inquisitions, religious wars and massacres, burning of heretics and forced ceremonies of worship, suicide bombers and pogroms, that the words of a fourteen-year-old boy stand as a light against all those dark shadows.

"Having been forbidden to join any of the religious sects of the day, and being of very tender years, and persecuted *by those who ought to have been my friends and to have treated me kindly, and if they supposed me to be deluded to have endeavored in a proper and affectionate manner to have reclaimed me*—I was left. . . ." (JS–H 1:28; emphasis added). How Joseph's words shine from the page: Friends. Kindly. Proper. Affectionate. The Savior's injunction was to seek the lost sheep, not to burn them or drive them deeper into the wilderness. How would the sad, suffering history of this world be changed if all those who claimed to act for God were guided by the compelling truth of a fourteen-year-old boy's words, especially towards those they supposed to be deluded?

HARMONY
AND THE
SUSQUEHANNA
RIVER

I AM ALWAYS A LITTLE DISAPPOINTED when I arrive at Harmony. The large cut of the railroad through the green bordering forest surrounding the Susquehanna River seems out of place considering the reverent realities that took place here. But once past its iron rails and seated by the river, the memories of the land awake, and I'm with Joseph again in the early 1800s.

Harmony is a place of pain and elation, as almost all places associated with the Prophet Joseph are. Here he received the severe rebuke when Martin Harris lost the 116 pages, a rebuke that was undoubtedly delivered by Moroni and is

Harmony Pennsylvania

As I drove through Pennsylvania trying to find Harmony, I wasn't on the kind of quiet buggy path portrayed in this painting—instead, I was speeding along an interstate highway. Even so, the scenery was so beautiful that I became engrossed and almost drove across the state line. This piece portrays my vision of what the Susquehanna looked like during those monumental days in Church history.

Al Rounds

recorded in Section 3 of the Doctrine and Covenants. Here he and Emma buried their first child, whose grave can still be seen. Yet in Harmony he loved Emma, courted her, and found in her one who would "comfort [him] in his afflictions, with consoling words, in the spirit of meekness" (D&C 25:5). It was a role given to Emma by the Lord Himself in the tiny frame home Joseph and Emma shared, whose foundations now lay buried under a small mound of earth.

Joseph's father would visit, and Joseph received for him a revelation, now memorized by every missionary. It contains the spirit of the Restoration inherent in three simple words: *marvelous, desires,* and *qualify.* (See D&C Section 4.) This work is marvelous and wonderful! If we have desires to help the Lord with it, He will allow us to participate, and we are called to the work. Service is not a burden, but a privilege—and we must qualify by attaining the highest virtues of Christianity.

Among the visitors who shared the tiny home was Oliver Cowdery, and with his arrival the translation of the Book of Mormon commenced in earnest. "These were days never to be forgotten," he wrote, "to sit under the sound of a voice dictated by the inspiration of heaven, awakened the utmost gratitude of this bosom!" (JS–H Footnote). Oliver, too, wanted to translate, and his failure gives to us the greatest understanding of what was required of Joseph—what labor took place in the little home by the river. "Behold, you have not understood;" the Lord told him, "you have supposed that I would give it unto you, when you took no thought save it was to ask me. But, behold, I say unto you, that you must *study it out in your mind . . .* " (D&C 9:7–8; emphasis added). There is the key—the mental exertion demanded of translation, the creation of the right words and phrases in English that captured the ideas that the Urim and Thummin revealed to him from the Nephite records.

It is always pleasant to sit by the Susquehanna and watch the water flowing softly past the bluffs on the other side. It is a suitable setting for the return of John the Baptist, whose life was so associated with a river—the Jordan. Now he would come to another, in the

I seem to see the bluff on the opposite shore lined with thousands and tens of thousands of the souls of the dead who came to watch this turning point in history.

Oliver Cowdery
on the visit of John the Baptist

You will believe me when I say, that earth, nor men, with the eloquence of time, cannot begin to clothe language in as interesting and sublime a manner as this holy personage. No; nor has this earth the power to give the joy, to bestow the peace, or comprehend the wisdom which was contained in each sentence as they were delivered by the power of the Holy Spirit! . . . The assurance that we were in the presence of an angel, the certainty that we heard the voice of Jesus, and the truth unsullied as it flowed from a pure personage, dictated by the will of God, is to me past description, and I shall ever look upon this expression of the Savior's goodness with wonder and thanksgiving. . . (JS–H Footnote).

wilderness of America, and restore the priesthood that the greatest work of the latter days could in time commence. He told Joseph and Oliver that it would "never be taken again from the earth, until the sons of Levi do offer again an offering unto the Lord in righteousness" (D&C 13:1).

I am sure they did not comprehend all that the Baptist's words encompassed, but as the Restoration unfolded "line upon line," the reality of John's promise became apparent. In Nauvoo, quoting the same Malachi prophecy spoken to Joseph as he knelt at the feet of the baptizer of the Savior, Joseph wrote, "Let us, therefore, as a church and a people, and as Latter-day Saints, offer unto the Lord an offering in righteousness; and let us present in his holy temple, when it is finished, a book containing the records of our dead, which shall be worthy of all acceptation" (D&C 128:24). So it was baptism for the dead the Baptist had centered in his mind as he laid his hands on the living.

I read those lines each time I come to the Susquehanna, and I envision the solitary scene of three men—two living and one resurrected—performing ordinances in the shallow water. But then that scene changes. I seem to see the bluff on the opposite shore lined with thousands and tens of thousands of the souls of the dead who came to watch this turning point in history. The restoration of the priesthood was taking place, an event that would culminate in the great temple ordinances for which so many of them had waited for centuries. I feel their elation as the veil thins; time becomes inconsequential, the present melts into the past and merges with the future in one great celebration of joy. Of the many sacred spaces of the history of this Church, the banks of the Susquehanna have always been for me where the voice of gladness for the living and the dead seems to ring with highest intensity. "Let the . . . rivers . . . flow down with gladness," Joseph later wrote (D&C 128:23). We may still hear that gladness in the quiet waters on the banks of the Susquehanna.

WHITMER CABIN IN FAYETTE

VARIOUS PLACES ALONG THE CHURCH HISTORY TRAIL have strong associations with very specific emotions. For me, Fayette always brings to mind the emotional quality of mercy. Though it was here that the Church was officially organized, it is to the Three Witnesses that my heart turns whenever I arrive and walk through the Peter Whitmer cabin and into the surrounding woods. In this cabin the final translation work was finished, and the Book of Mormon was ready to make its debut on the stage of scriptural history. However, the Lord does not break His own rules, and one of them is the need for multiple witnesses.

It is indicative of the Lord's nature that in spite of Martin Harris's loss of 116 pages of sacred script, he was still chosen by a merciful God to be one of the prophesied witnesses. One could make a very convincing case for others, but

Peter Whitmer Cabin

In late June 1829, Joseph Smith completed the translation of the Book of Mormon here. In nearby woods, the Three Witnesses saw the angel Moroni and the gold plates. On 6 April 1830, about 60 people assembled at the Peter Whitmer home to witness the formal organization of the Church of Jesus Christ of Latter-day Saints.

Martin was to receive his desires—a recompense for his sacrifices and goodness rather than exclusion for his weakness and folly. Lucy Mack Smith's account of the moment Martin was selected carries the appropriate spirit. "Joseph arose from his knees, and approaching Martin Harris with a solemnity that thrills through my veins to this day . . . said, 'Martin Harris, you have got to humble yourself before God this day that you may obtain a forgiveness of your sins. If you do, it is the will of God that you should look upon the plates'" (Lucy Mack Smith, 152).

Retreating into the woods, the four men prayed, but failed to receive a divine manifestation until Martin left the quartet. Moroni then appeared to the three remaining young men and showed to them the Nephite records. Searching out Martin, Joseph knelt again in prayer with his broken-hearted and contrite older friend. "We . . . ultimately obtained our desires . . . " Joseph said, "and I once more beheld and heard the same things; whilst at the same moment, Martin Harris cried out, apparently in an ecstasy of joy, 'Tis enough; 'tis enough; mine eyes have beheld; mine eyes have beheld'; and jumping up, he shouted, 'Hosanna,' blessing God, and otherwise rejoiced exceedingly" (*History of the Church* 1:55).

"Who can say too much of . . . his mercy, and of his long-suffering towards the children of men?" Ammon once asked. "I cannot say the

David Whitmer
witness of the plates

Joseph, and Oliver and I were sitting just here on a log, when we were overshadowed by a light . . . glorious and beautiful. . . . In the midst of this light . . . appeared, as it were, a table with many records or plates, . . . also the sword of Laban, the directors. . . . I saw just as plain as I see this bed and I heard the voice of the Lord, as distinctly as I ever heard anything in my life, declaring that the records of the plates of the Book of Mormon were translated by the gift and the power of God." *(Kansas City Journal,* June 5, 1881; Andrew Jensen, *LDS Biographical Encyclopedia* [Salt Lake City: The Deseret News, 1901], 266.)

Fayette always brings to mind the emotional quality of mercy.

smallest part which I feel" (Alma 26:16). "It is of the Lord's mercies . . . " Jeremiah taught, "because his compassions fail not. They are new every morning. . . " (Lam. 3:22–23). Being the recipient of such goodness, Martin would add his own testimony of the Lord's mercy: "I bless God in the sincerity of my soul that he has condescended to make me, even me, a witness of the greatness of his work."

Though Martin is known as a witness of golden plates, in perhaps an equally profound way, he was witness to the patient kindness of Christ's mercy. When he lost the 116 pages of manuscript, Martin was called a "wicked man" by the Lord. (See D&C Sections 3 and 10.) Notice he was not called a "weak" man, but a wicked one. The words sound harsh, but it makes the events of Fayette even more tender. He had gone from "wicked man" to witness in the openly forgiving perspective of God's world. Perhaps Martin thought that all was lost in those frantic, searching, fear-filled moments when the realization pounded home that the precious writings were gone. In the Smith kitchen in Palmyra he had cried "in a tone of deep anguish, 'Oh, I have lost my soul! I have lost

Martin Harris Farmhouse

This image depicts a victorian home still standing on the property formerly owned by Martin Harris in Palmyra, New York.

Martin Harris Farm

My goal with this painting was to portray the success of Martin Harris, a man whose diligent labor and excellent management made his a high-yielding farm of 320 acres in Palmyra, New York. The bounties of that hard work put him in a unique position to be of financial assistance to the Restoration, a blessing for which we owe a debt of gratitude today. When the Book of Mormon was completed, Joseph Smith had trouble finding a printer who would undertake the publication. A Palmyra printer was finally found only after Martin mortgaged his farm for $3000 as security. _____

my soul!'" (Lucy Mack Smith, 128). But God's ways are not our ways, and the lost soul was found and blessed and trusted anew in the woods by the Peter Whitmer farm—woods made holy by that one act of redemptive mercy that was more than mere forgiveness.

The day was also one of kindness and benevolence to Joseph, who had carried the heavy burden of single testimony from that first autumn night in the Smith log home when he "discovered a light appearing in my room. . . " (JS–H 1:30). As he returned with his three newly chosen, weight-bearing pillars of witness he "threw himself down beside me," his mother wrote, "and exclaimed, 'Father, mother, you do not know how happy I am: The Lord has now caused the plates to be shown to three more besides myself. They have seen an angel, who has testified to them, and they will have to bear witness to the truth of what I have said, for now they know for themselves that I do not go about to deceive the people, and I feel as if I was relieved of a burden which was almost too heavy for me to bear, and it rejoices my soul, that I am not any longer to be entirely alone in the world" (Lucy Mack Smith, 152).

Kirtland

PROPHECY
GIVEN NEAR THE ISAAC MORLEY FARM

City Creek Canyon Sunset

This painting captures the view from City Creek Canyon in Salt Lake at sunset. While the rest of the valley reposes in shadow, a ray of light from the setting sun illuminates Temple Square with a heavenly glow—a phenomenon that happens only in the summer months, when the sun peeks between the Oquirrh Mountains and the ridges of Antelope Island.

Kirtland Temple

Previous page: I'll never forget my first trip to the Church history sites—I spent an entire month on the road, camping out where I could and finding greater awe and appreciation with each new discovery. Of all the work I did that month, this was the first time the brush touched canvas. The painting later won an award in a Church art competition and was featured on the cover of the March 1980 Ensign magazine.

THE SPOT MOST DEAR TO MY HEART in Kirtland is one I was only allowed to visit once. It is the site of the old log schoolhouse above the Isaac Morley farm. I have visited the farm many times and have walked the short path up the hill to the place where it ends at private property—the ground upon which the old schoolhouse stood. There I have contemplated the memory of my visit when permission was granted and I stood where Joseph had once stood during the dark days of the Jackson County persecutions when the grand design of building Zion was threatened. Joseph gathered the priesthood leadership of the Church who were then in Kirtland into the schoolhouse for a testimony meeting. In the confined space were Oliver Cowdery, Brigham Young, Heber C. Kimball, the Pratt brothers, Orson Hyde, and others. Years later, Wilford Woodruff related the experience that then ensued:

"It was a small house, perhaps 14 feet square. . . . When we got together the Prophet called upon the Elders of Israel with him to bear testimony of this work. Those that I have named spoke, and a good many that I have not named, bore their testimonies. When they got through the Prophet said: 'Brethren I have been very much edified and instructed in your testimonies here tonight, but I want to say to you before the Lord, that you know no more concerning the destinies of this Church and kingdom than a babe upon its mother's lap. You don't comprehend it. . . . It is only a little handfull of Priesthood you see here tonight, but this Church will fill North and South America—it will fill the world. . . . It will fill the Rocky Mountains. There will be tens of thousands of Latter-day Saints who will be gathered in the Rocky Mountains. . . . They will there build temples to the Most High. They will raise up a posterity there, and the Latter-day Saints . . . will stand in the flesh until the coming of the Son of Man" (*Conference Report,* April 8, 1898, 57).

As I stood there, the Spirit took hold of my imagination. I could see the little band with Joseph at their head. He seemed tired, weary with the load he was asked to carry. I was overcome with feeling for him. I felt like saying to him, "Joseph, I'm from the future. Don't be discouraged. We have twelve million members, hundreds of missions, tens of thousands of missionaries. There are temples all over the world. The gospel is being preached in many, many lands." As I finished, Joseph seemed to pause, turn his head slightly in my direction, and a faint hint of a smile touched his lips. He seemed to say to me, "I know. I have seen it all. In truth, you of the future have no more idea of the destinies of this Church than a babe upon its mother's lap. You don't comprehend it."

WHITNEY STORE AND JOHNSON FARM

Kirtland at a Distance

Around the turn of the century, photographer George Edward Anderson set off for a mission in England; on his way, he stopped in Kirtland and shot a stunning series of pictures. Early in my career I went to Kirtland determined to duplicate his perspective. Imagine my reverence when I found that he had to climb trees—and even break branches—to capture such spectacular views.

JOHN RUSKIN ONCE SAID, "Great nations write their autobiographies in three manuscripts—the book of their deeds, the book of their words, and the book of their art." What is true of great nations is also true of great religions—even great individuals. I am not sure we can rank Ruskin's three books in order of importance, but for me personally it is the book of words that distinguishes with such clarity the depth and dignity of a man, a religion, or a nation.

When I come to Kirtland and visit the Whitney Store and the John Johnson Home my mind is always drawn to the great words that proceeded from these completely ordinary buildings. Almost one-half of all the sections in the Doctrine and Covenants were revealed in Kirtland, and the majority of those were revealed in the Whitney Store and on the Johnson Farm, along with the Morley Farm. If there is validation for our faith in the prophetic power of Joseph Smith, it rests in the glorious words and profound ideas he penned. Parley P.

CONSIDER SOME OF THE TRUTHS FROM THE "BOOK OF WORDS" COMPRISING JOSEPH SMITH'S LEGACY TO US ALL:

And now, after the many testimonies which have been given of him, this is the testimony, last of all, which we give of him: That he lives! For we saw him, even on the right hand of God . . . (D&C 76:22–23)

The glory of God is intelligence, or, in other words, light and truth. (D&C 93:36)

SEEK YE DILIGENTLY

and teach one another

WORDS OF WISDOM;

yea, seek ye out of the best books words of wisdom; **SEEK LEARNING,** even by study and also by faith.

(D&C 88:118)

For you shall live by every word that proceedeth forth from the mouth of God. (D&C 84:44)

Let Zion rejoice, for this is

ZION

THE PURE IN HEART

(D&C 97:21)

In the day of their peace they esteemed lightly my counsel; but, in the day of their trouble, of necessity they feel after me.

(D&C 101:8)

AND FOR THIS CAUSE, THAT MEN MIGHT BE MADE PARTAKERS OF THE GLORIES WHICH WERE TO BE REVEALED, THE LORD SENT FORTH THE FULNESS OF HIS GOSPEL, HIS EVERLASTING COVENANT, REASONING IN PLAINNESS AND SIMPLICITY.

(D&C 133:57)

Pratt described how many of these influential words were transferred from the heavens to the mind of Joseph and then to all of us:

"Each sentence was uttered slowly and very distinctly, and with a pause between each, sufficiently long for it to be recorded, by an ordinary writer, in long hand.

"This was the manner in which all his written revelations were dictated and written. There was never any hesitation, reviewing, or reading back, in order to keep the run of the subject; neither did any of these communications undergo revisions, interlinings, or corrections. As he dictated them so they stood, so far as I have witnessed; and I was present to witness the dictation of several communications of several pages each" (Parley P. Pratt, *Autobiography of Parley P. Pratt* [Salt Lake City: Deseret Book, 1938], 62).

My faith is always confirmed when I sit under a tree at the Johnson Farm or on the porch of the Whitney Store after walking through their tiny rooms, reading section after section of the Doctrine and Covenants. There are so many sections to choose from—Sections 1, 68, 76, 78, 84, 87, 88, 89, 93, 97, 98, 101, 133. This is just the beginning. From these simple rooms came the Word of Wisdom, gifts of the Spirit, the Law of Consecration, the Three Degrees of Glory, the war in heaven, the Olive Leaf, the nature of intelligence, the Oath and Covenant of the Priesthood, the gifts and power of the temple, the inspired nature of the Constitution, the leading quorums of the Church, the Second Coming of Christ, and dozens more, too numerous to list.

While walking through the elegant splendor of the Hall of Mirrors at the Palace of Versailles outside Paris, I recalled hearing that a man remarked that nothing of real consequence for the betterment and advancement of man had ever taken place in a large room. It is not in the grandiose, the elegant, the ostentatious, or pretentious that God works His wonders, but in the simple, the plain, and the unobtrusive. In the tiny village of Kirtland, within the cramped confines of farmhouses and country stores, the majestic truths of eternity were unfolded. As God Himself revealed there, "the weak things of the world shall come forth and break down the mighty and strong ones," and that He could humble

Letter from *Joseph Smith* to William W. Phelps

Oh, Lord, when will the time come when Brother William, Thy servant, and myself, shall behold the day that we may stand together and gaze upon eternal wisdom engraven upon the heavens, while the majesty of our God holdeth up the dark curtain until we may read the round of eternity, to the fullness and satisfaction of our immortal souls? Oh, Lord, deliver us in due time from the little, narrow prison, almost as it were, total darkness of paper, pen and ink;—and a crooked, broken, scattered and imperfect language.

(History of the Church 1:299.)

What fascinates me is that mobs would travel that kind of distance to persecute humble, God-fearing people.

"kings and rulers" by the "weak and the simple" (D&C 1:19, 23). Surrounded by the commonplace, we need not be limited by the mundane. We can follow the Lord's invitation, given in the first weeks of Joseph's arrival in Kirtland: "Treasure these things up in your hearts and let the solemnities of eternity rest upon your minds" (D&C 43:34).

Joseph once said, "It is my meditation all the day, and more than my meat and drink, to know how I shall make the Saints of God comprehend the visions that roll like an overflowing surge before my mind" (*Teachings of the Prophet Joseph Smith,* 296). However, there was a cost to be paid for the precious pearls of truth flowing through the mind of Joseph. One night's fearful experience is sufficient to understand that price. On Saturday, March 24, 1832, while Joseph was sleeping at the Johnson Farm, a mob broke into the house, dragged him several hundred yards, beat and scratched him, and tried to force a vial of poison between his clenched teeth. Afterwards they tarred and feathered him and left him to stumble his way back to the house in the darkness. But the "surge" of truth rolling through his mind could not be held back. Throughout the rest of the night Emma removed the tar; Joseph later reported, "With my flesh all scarified and defaced, I preached to the congregation as usual, and in the afternoon of the same day baptized three individuals" (*History of the Church,* 1:264).

John Johnson Farm

I am intrigued to this day by how far the John Johnson Farm is from the center of Kirtland, the hub of most commercial and residential activity and the site upon which the Saints built the temple. This farm is located in Hiram, approximately thirty miles from Kirtland. But what fascinates me even more is the fact that despite all that had to be done to support a family in those times—tilling the ground, tending the crops, feeding the animals, and making much by hand—the mobs still found the time and energy to travel that kind of distance to persecute humble, God-fearing people.

KIRTLAND TEMPLE

THE CROWN OF KIRTLAND IS THE TEMPLE, the first to be built in this dispensation. How remarkable that it is still standing for us to visit and enjoy, considering the apostasy, mob violence, and abandonment. Built in the Saints' poverty, it is the major legacy of a believing people and a testament of their devotion to God. To me it is a symbol of how to find peace in a world continually beset by conflict.

The Lord commanded the Church in Kirtland to build Him a house in Section 88 of the Doctrine and Covenants. The relevancy of the temple is seen to an even greater degree when we examine the two sections immediately preceding the Lord's command that a temple be built.

Section 86 is an interpretation of the Savior's parable of the wheat and the tares. It deals with an apostate world. In the darkness of apostasy the locusts

Kirtland Reflections

This painting beautifully captures the Kirtland Temple as reflected in the Chagrin River. This river was the location for many baptisms in the early Church and is described in several journals.

of war are born. This leads us to Section 87, titled "The Prophecy on War." There is a natural connection between the two sections. In Section 87 Joseph Smith foretold the coming Civil War. But he went further than that, stating, "the time will come that war will be poured out upon all nations. . . " (D&C 87:2). Those wars "will eventually terminate in the death and misery of many souls" (D&C 87:1).

We have seen the fulfillment of these words and continue to see it. What is remarkable and inspiring of hope is Section 88, titled The Olive Leaf, "plucked from the Tree of Paradise, the Lord's message of peace to us" (heading to Section 88). Within its verses we discover the means of finding peace even in a world spiraling deeper and

Lucy Mack Smith on building the temple

Some were in favor of building a frame house, but others were of a mind to put up a log house. Joseph reminded them that they were not building a house for a man, but for God; "and shall we brethren," said he, "build a house for our God, of logs? No, I have a better plan than that. I have a plan of the house of the Lord, given by himself; and you will soon see by this, the difference between our calculations and his idea of things. (Lucy Mack Smith, 230.)

deeper into destructive conflicts. The center of that peace is the holy temple. In fact, Section 87 ends with the command to "stand ye in holy places, and be not moved" (D&C 87:8). What holier place can we find than the Lord's house?

When I sit on the benches of the Kirtland Temple, I think of the Lord's own description of what it was meant to be—"a house of prayer, a house of fasting, a house of faith, a house of learning, a house of glory, a house of order, a house of God" (D&C 88:119). Not to build the temple or avail oneself of its proffered blessings was tantamount to "walking in darkness at noon-day" (D&C 95:6). "Now here is wisdom, and the mind of the Lord—let the house be built . . . for I give not unto you that ye shall live after the manner of the world" (D&C 95:13). Here was a place for "offering up of your most holy desires unto me" (D&C 95:16). The center of a Zion people, the key to their differentiation from worldliness and the refinement of their holiest desires, lay in the temple and its ordinances. I wonder: Could the early Saints have understood the power of what they were building?

Sitting before the multiple pulpits on the main floor, one can almost hear the majestic prayer once offered by the Prophet Joseph Smith, dedicating the Saints' efforts to their Savior and enumerating the temple's promised blessings. The phrases wash with a cleansing healing over one's soul as the troubles of an angry world are soothed away. "The Son of Man might have a place to manifest himself to his people. . . . " "Thy glory may rest down upon thy people. . . ."

"Thy holy presence may be continually in this house. . . . " "All people who shall enter upon the threshold of the Lord's house may feel thy power. . . . " "All those who shall worship in this house may be taught words of wisdom out of the best books. . . . " "They may grow up in thee, and receive a fullness of the Holy Ghost, and be organized according to thy laws, and be prepared to obtain every needful thing. . . . " "Thy servants may go forth from this house armed with thy power . . . and thy glory be round about them, and thine angels have charge over them. . . . " "Establish the people that shall worship . . . in this thy house . . . to all generations and for eternity. . . . " "No combination of wickedness shall have power to rise up and prevail over thy people upon whom thy name shall be put in this house. . . . " All this that the Lord's Church and people may "come forth out of the wilderness of darkness, and shine forth fair as the moon, clear as the sun . . . adorned as a bride. . . . that we may ever be with the Lord." I have never left the Kirtland Temple without the feeling that all will be well, for our God dwells in "an infinity of fullness" and has provided holy places for our refuge. (See D&C 109: 5–26, 73–77.)

Kirtland Village

"Kirtland Village" beautifully captures the earliest Mormon settlement in Kirtland, Ohio, by depicting (from left to right) Sidney Gilbert's Home, Newell K. Whitney's Store, and Sidney Rigdon's Tannery. In the fall of 1832, Joseph Smith moved from Hiram, Ohio, back to Kirtland. Bishop Newel K. Whitney prepared an apartment for the Prophet's family in his store, and Joseph lived here until the winter of the following year. The Whitney Store served as headquarters for the Church during that time, including the School of the Prophets, which was held in an upper room during that winter. The Prophet received many revelations while staying here, including the Word of Wisdom and the command to build the Kirtland Temple.

To not build a temple or avail oneself of its proffered blessings was tantamount to "walking in darkness at noon-day."

A house of Glory . . .
A house of God

Joseph's prayer was answered by an outpouring of the Spirit witnessed by many in attendance that day. It was answered to a deeper degree by the appearance of the Savior Himself as Joseph and Oliver prayed within the enclosed confines of the pulpit while the curtains were dropped. They heard the words we all long to hear. We, too, can hear those words as we seek the Lord in prayer in any temple constructed and dedicated since that first outpouring of devoted labor: "Behold, your sins are forgiven you; you are clean before me; therefore, lift up your heads and rejoice" (D&C 110:5).

Kirtland Winter

In painting the Kirtland Temple as seen from Newell K. Whitney's Mill, I hoped to symbolize the importance of each to the community. Each was the lifeblood of the settlement—the temple providing spiritual life, and the mill providing the means for food, clothing, lumber, and the homes and stores that were built. I also hoped to symbolize that despite each one's importance, both were freely sacrificed by people who loved their God and who were willing to follow His injunction to leave Kirtland behind.

Missouri

OPPOSITION IN INDEPENDENCE

Independence, Missouri

Previous Page: Along this road are shown the courthouse and jail in Independence, Missouri. In November 1838 Joseph Smith and several Church leaders were held in this jail for several days. Eventually they were taken to Richmond and then Carthage Jail.

ALL GREAT CIVILIZATIONS OR MOVEMENTS IN HISTORY have drawn energy for their progress by their linkage with something noble in the past coupled with a sense of destiny towards the future. In America, the Founding Fathers felt they were the inheritors of the Greek and Roman worlds; evidence of that belief is seen in the architecture of Washington, D.C. Yet they were also inspired by the belief that they were establishing a pattern of freedom and liberty that would eventually encompass the world. Every school child has read about "manifest destiny."

This pattern is also obvious in the Church. Joseph Smith called us "Saints," reflecting the early Christians. We believe we are the "children of Israel," and our patriarchal blessings assure us that we are. These two ideas link us with both the Old and the New Testament traditions. Our heritage is long and noble.

As for a sense of destiny, shortly after finishing the Book of Mormon, Joseph received the revelations we know as the Book of Moses. Contained within its narratives is the story of Enoch and the building

personal writings of *Mary Lightner*

The mob renewed their efforts again by tearing down the printing office, a two story building, and driving Brother Phelps' family out of the lower part of the house and putting their things in the street. They brought out some large sheets of paper, and said, "Here are the Mormon Commandments." My sister Caroline and myself were in a corner of a fence watching them; when they spoke of the commandments I was determined to have some of them. Sister said if I went to get any of them she would go too, but said "They will kill us." While their backs were turned, prying out the gable end of the house, we went, and got our arms full, and were turning away, when some of the mob saw us and called on us to stop, but we ran as fast as we could. Two of them started after us. Seeing a gap in a fence, we entered into a large cornfield, laid the papers on the ground, and hid them with our persons. The corn was from five to six feet high, and very thick; they hunted around considerable, and came very near us but did not find us. . . . They got them bound in small books and sent me one, which I prized very highly. ("Autobiography of Mary Lightner," *Utah Genealogical and Historical Magazine* 17 (1926), 196–97.)

of Zion—a city so pleasing to God that He took it to Himself because its citizens were too righteous to remain in a decadent world. The concept of building a Zion society, the New Jerusalem, became the compelling belief that drove the Church forward. Almost immediately after receiving the revelations on Enoch, the idea of Zion began to appear in the Doctrine and Covenants, and Missouri was where the dream began.

I cannot help but think of this when exploring the Church history sites in Missouri, particularly those in Independence. The scope of Joseph's horizons was vast, and he infused his own visionary enthusiasm into the hearts of his followers. Enoch's city was described as being of "one heart and one mind" with "no poor among them" (Moses 7:18). Consecration would be the engine to create the oneness.

But two barriers stood in the way. Independence was at the rugged edges of the American frontier and its citizens were equally raw. Opposition started almost from the building of the first log cabin. The Lord revealed the coming storm the first week of their arrival.

"For after much tribulation come the blessings. . . . Remember this, which I tell you before, that you may lay it to heart, and receive that which is to follow" (D&C 58:4–5). They were ominous words for the beginning of Zion.

Though the mind can agree, and even be inspired with zeal for the enterprise, the frailties and weakness of mortal man—even the best of men—are challenging to overcome. How do you all become one when so much of our natures cry against it? As a result, there were "jarrings, and contentions . . . and covetous desires among them; therefore, by these things they polluted their inheritances" (D&C 101:6).

I cannot blame them or find deep fault. They were new converts, pulsing with zeal, but inexperienced and prone to habitual modes of thinking that so often gravitate to the self. It is interesting that through all the warnings and explanations concerning the Jackson County persecutions, the Lord does not lay the blame at the feet of the mob, but at those of the Saints. Not that they caused it, but because of their inability to live the laws of a Zion people "I, the Lord, have suffered the affliction to come upon them . . . " (D&C 101:2).

The concept of building a Zion society, the New Jerusalem, became the compelling belief that drove the Church forward.

Whittingham, Vermont

Whittingham, Vermont, is the birthplace of the Prophet Brigham Young in 1801. Brigham Young was the ninth of eleven children, and he lived in Whittingham until he was three years old. A monument has now been placed on the original site of the Whittingham Village to mark his birthplace.

I suppose the Lord knew the final outcome from the beginning, but He lets His children reach for the heights. Their disappointments have provided valuable lessons for us, who are still under the injunction to build Zion. One thing is clear: a major part of their failure is symbolized by the empty temple plot in downtown Independence. I have walked across it often, reading the Jackson County revelations, particularly Section 97, given even as the persecutions began to rage:

"It is my will that a house should be built unto me in the land of Zion. . . . Yea, let it be *built speedily.* . . . for a place of thanksgiving for all saints, and for a place of instruction . . . *that they may be perfected . . . in all things pertaining to the kingdom of God on the earth.*

The center of Zion must be the temple.

. . . If Zion do these things she shall prosper, and spread herself and become very glorious, very great . . . and the nations of the earth shall honor her, and shall say: Surely Zion is the city of our God" (D&C 97:10–19; emphasis added).

The Lord had told them earlier that the center of Zion must be the temple. "The city New Jerusalem shall be built by the gathering of the saints, beginning at this place, even the place of the temple. . ." (D&C 84:4). Jesus taught that if we are not one, we are not His disciples, and that Zion is a one heart, one mind people. It is in the House of the Lord that the chains of oneness are forged in the white heat of its ordinances—husband to wife, parent to child, saint to saint, living to dead, and man with God. So many words and actions associated with temple worship encompass the idea of unity and oneness.

After a number of opportunities to redeem Zion through things like Zion's Camp, the Lord indicated, "it is expedient in me that mine elders should wait for a little season for the redemption of Zion— That they themselves may be prepared, and *that my people may be taught more perfectly, and have experience, and know more perfectly concerning their duty,* and the things which I require at their hands. *And this cannot be brought to pass until mine elders are endowed with power from on high.* For behold, I have prepared a great endowment and blessing to be poured out upon them. . . " (D&C 105:9–12; emphasis added).

The dedicated spot for the temple in Independence still lies empty. I never leave it without a solemn appreciation for the temples that now stand, into which I am privileged to enter to receive experience and to be instructed "more perfectly" in all things that pertain to the Lord's kingdom. I never leave it without profound gratitude for those early Saints, who first picked up their axes and shovels and strived in the face of their own weaknesses to create a perfected Zion people. Are we doing any better?

FAR WEST

FOR ME, FAR WEST IS A PLACE OF VOICES—solemn, sobering voices. Whenever I visit, I can hear them still reverberating through the grass and over the prairie. They speak of different things.

There is the voice of betrayal as Colonel Hinkle delivered Joseph, Hyrum, and others into the hands of the mob leader, General Lucas: "Here, general, are the prisoners I agreed to deliver to you" (*History of the Church* 3:445).

There is the tragically imprudent voice of Jacob Haun rejecting Joseph's counsel to move into Far West, confident that the Saints at Haun's Mill could defend themselves by using the blacksmith shop as a fortification. There is Joseph's concerned voice when he departed: "That man did not come to me for counsel, but to induce me to tell him to do as he pleased; which I did. Had I commanded them to move in here and leave their property, they would have called me a tyrant. I wish they were here for their own safety" (John D. Lee, *Mormonism Unveiled: The Life and Confessions of John D. Lee* [Albuquerque, New Mexico: University of New Mexico Press, 2001], 88).

Al Rounds ©85

Far West is a place of voices—those of pain and fear,
but also those of courage, loyalty, integrity, and faith.

There is the terrified voice of Joseph Smith's son recorded in the Doctrine and Covenants as he saw his father arrested: *"My father, my father, why can't you stay with us? O, my father, what are the men going to do with you?"* (D&C 122:6; emphasis added). There is the voice of Parley P. Pratt taking leave of his family on his way to jail with Joseph Smith: "I went to my house . . . the cold rain was pouring down without, and on entering my little cottage, there lay my wife sick of a fever. . . . I stepped to the bed; my wife burst into tears . . . " (Pratt, 189).

There is the taunting voice of Major–General Clark speaking to the frightened citizens of the city: "As for your leaders, do not think, do not imagine for a moment, do not let it enter your mind that they will be delivered, or that you will see their faces again, for their fate is fixed, their die is cast, their doom is sealed" (Pratt, 208). The voice of Lucy Mack Smith is one of the most poignant as she struggled through the mob to see her sons: "Joseph, do speak to your poor mother once more—I cannot bear to go till I hear your voice" (Lucy Mack Smith, 291).

So many voices! Yet among those of pain and fear, I hear the voices of courage, born of loyalty, integrity, and faith. Because of these voices, Far West will always remain in my mind a place of valor.

I hear the voice of Lyman Wight when offered his freedom by Moses Wilson if he would turn against Joseph Smith. "'Wight,' Wilson said, 'you're a strange

Far West

This contemporary view of the temple site in Far West, Missouri, probably doesn't differ much from the desolated site that existed when the Saints dedicated it for the building of a temple. One is struck with both sorrow and awe—sorrow that mobs desecrated this site with their murderous rage, claiming hundreds of lives and leaving thousands more homeless, and awe that a faithful people could gaze upon such desolation and envision it as the future center of Zion.

Heber C. Kimball
on laying the cornerstone for the Far West Temple

I kept myself concealed in the woods and passed round the country, notifying the brethren and sisters to be on hand at the appointed time for the laying of the cornerstone. April 25. This night, which was a beautiful, clear moonlight, Elders Brigham Young, Orson Pratt, John E. Page, John Taylor, Wilford Woodruff, George A. Smith and Alpheus Cutler, arrived from Quincy, Illinois, and rode into the public square early on the morning of the 26. All seemed still as death. . . . [We] proceeded to the building spot of the Lord's house, where, after singing, we [recommenced] laying the foundation, agreeably to the revelation given July 8, 1838, by rolling a stone, upwards of a ton weight, upon or near the southeast corner. . . . The brethren wandered among our deserted houses, many of which were in ruins, and saw the streets in many places grown over with weeds and grass. (Orson F. Whitney, *Life of Heber C. Kimball* [Salt Lake City: Bookcraft, 1945], 252–53.)

man. But if you do not accept my proposal, you will be shot tomorrow at nine.' And Lyman answered: 'Shoot and be d—d'" (Hyrum Andrus, *Joseph Smith, the Man and the Seer* [Salt Lake City: Deseret Book, 1960], 44).

There is the voice of Alexander Doniphan who, when ordered to shoot the prisoners by General Lucas, replied: "It is cold-blooded murder. I will not obey your order. My brigade shall march for Liberty tomorrow morning at 8 o'clock; and if you execute those men, I will hold you responsible before an earthly tribunal, so help me God!" (Ivan J. Barrett, *Joseph Smith and the Restoration* [Provo, Utah: Brigham Young University Press, 1982], 405).

And there are the courageous voices of Brigham Young, Heber C. Kimball, John Taylor, Wilford Woodruff, and others of the Twelve who, in spite of threats from mobs and apostates, returned in the dead of night to the temple plot in Far West to lay the southeast cornerstone of the temple before leaving for their missions to England as asked of the Lord: "Let them take leave of my saints in the city of Far West, on the twenty-sixth day of April next, on the building-spot of my house, saith the Lord" (D&C 118:5).

The voices of Far West are lonely voices that reveal all that is best and worst in man. They echo still, encouraging us and sobering us with the memories of the land.

ADAM-ONDI-AHMAN

Lyman Wight Cabin

While the majority of the Saints settled in the "Mormon County" of Caldwell, a few of the Saints, including Lyman Wight, also settled in Daviess County. He purchased a farm in February 1838, and operated a ferry on the Grand River. In May, while visiting Lyman Wight, Joseph received the revelation that Spring Hill was actually Adam-ondi-Ahman.

THIS IS ALWAYS A FAVORITE STOP IN MY MISSOURI wanderings. However, it turns my thoughts to the future more powerfully than to the past. It is a place of hope, not only for the Saints, but for the world. "Spring Hill," Joseph revealed in the Doctrine and Covenants, "is named by the Lord Adam-ondi-Ahman, because, said he, it is the place where Adam shall come to visit his people, or the Ancient of Days shall sit, as spoken of by Daniel the prophet" (D&C 116:1).

One should never visit Spring Hill without turning to the seventh chapter of Daniel. Daniel saw the great empires of the world, metaphorically arising like beasts out of a chaotic sea torn by the fury of the wind. Mankind has been ruled by the law of the jungle for millenniums, but Daniel promised: "I beheld till the thrones were cast down, and the Ancient of days did sit. . . . ten thousand times ten thousand stood before him: the judgment was set, and the books were opened" (Dan. 7:9–10).

In the Garden of Eden, God gave to Adam dominion over all the earth, but his descendants have been fighting over that inheritance ever since. Yet, Adam will return one day to end the conflicts.

Edward Stephenson

In Missouri, when mob forces oppressed the Saints, we were encamped in Adam-ondi-Ahman, mostly around campfires without tents. One night the snow fell four or five inches. The Prophet, seeing our forlorn condition, called on us to form into two parties—Lyman Wight at the head of one line and he (Joseph) heading the other line—to have a sham battle. The weapons were snowballs. We set to with a will full of glee and fun. (Autobiography of Edward Stephenson, Manuscript in Church Historian's Library, Salt Lake City, Utah.)

_____Spring Hill

In this portrayal of Spring Hill the Lyman Wight cabin is situated in the background near the gently sloping crest of the hill.

Standing before the vast multitude of his children, he will ask, who among them all has shown he can rule the children of men in happiness, peace, and justice? The answer is obvious!

"I saw in the night visions, and, behold, one like the Son of man came with the clouds of heaven, and came to the Ancient of days. . . . And there was given him dominion, and glory, and a kingdom, that all people, nations, and languages, should serve him: his dominion is an everlasting dominion, which shall not pass away . . . " (Dan. 7:13–14). Only the Lord Jesus Christ is worthy of guiding the earth on the paths of peace and joy. He will one day do so with the help of the Saints. "The saints of the most High shall take the kingdom, and possess the kingdom for ever, even for ever and ever" (Dan. 7:18). How these words must have stirred the vigor of the early Saints as they stir us today! They were mighty ideas for a frontier church in a log cabin setting.

The flowing nature of the land, its gently rolling hills seem a just setting for such a beautiful prophecy—the ending of all conflicts in the meekness of the Son of God. There is a reverent solitude and calm here. It foreshadows the ultimate peace in which the whole world will one day rejoice. I always hesitate to depart, for here the discordant sounds of war and conquest will fade away in the reassuring quiet I always sense in the hills and valleys of Adam-ondi-Ahman.

LIBERTY JAIL

Liberty Jail Winter

This painting depicts winter at Liberty Jail, where Joseph Smith and others were unjustly imprisoned in the basement from December 1838 to April 1839 awaiting trial. Other Church leaders were incarcerated in Liberty Jail with Joseph: Hyrum Smith, Sidney Rigdon, Lyman Wight, Alexander McRae, and Caleb Baldwin. Because of the small slits in the walls that served as windows for their cell, they suffered from intense cold and exposure to the elements. They slept on dirty straw and suffered poisoning attempts and insults. However, Joseph's biggest grievance was not his own condition of imprisonment but the knowledge that the members of The Church of Jesus Christ of Latter-day Saints were suffering untold agonies that he could not prevent. Despite all the physical and emotional anguish he was suffering, Joseph received three revelations during this imprisonment that are recorded in the Doctrine and Covenants.

WHEN AT LIBERTY JAIL I ALWAYS READ the Savior's beautiful and comforting words to Joseph, "Know thou, my son, that all these things shall give thee experience, and shall be for thy good. The Son of Man hath descended below them all. Art thou greater than he?" (D&C 122:7-8). These words encompass the great message of relevancy that Liberty imparts for us all when we face our own dark hours. Yet other thoughts also come as I stare into the "pit" that was home to Joseph and Hyrum during the winter of 1838–39.

At Harmony, Joseph received a revelation for his wife, Emma. She desired to see the Nephite records, but God told her he had another "calling" in mind. He had eleven witnesses of the sacred plates; what He needed was a comforter for His prophet. "And the office of thy calling shall be for a comfort unto my servant, Joseph Smith, Jun., thy husband, in his afflictions, with consoling words, in the spirit of meekness" (D&C 25:5). Emma would fulfill this role throughout the life of Joseph Smith, but perhaps nowhere did she do it better than during those dark days of winter in the jail ironically called "Liberty."

Joseph penned a letter to the Saints from Liberty Jail from which we derive Sections 121–123 of the Doctrine and Covenants. We do not have the full letter in the scriptures, but it is instructive to read the entire letter, for therein we receive

Liberty Jail Spring

This painting depicts the jail in the springtime, when Joseph's ordeal was finally about to come to an end. In April 1839, Joseph and his fellow prisoners were transported to Gallatin, Missouri, for a grand jury hearing. At the end of the trial where Joseph and the others stood before a drunken jury, the prisoners were told they would be moved to the jail in Boone County. While traveling to Boone County under the guard of Sheriff William Morgan, Joseph and his company were allowed to escape from the guards, who then all became drunk. Because of their weakened condition, it took Joseph and his companions six days to arrive at Quincy, Illinois, to join the main body of the Church.

added insight. The poignant prayer at the beginning of Section 121 was preceded by a catalogue of the wrongs suffered by the Saints at the hands of Missouri. That context helps us establish the tone of Joseph's prayer as something much more agonized and desperate than commonly understood. The Lord responds to Joseph's "O God, where art thou?" with "My son, peace be unto thy soul. . . ." (D&C 121:1, 7). But the answer did not come until Joseph had received some letters that produced in him a change of soul. He related the impact of those letters on his troubled heart in the following words:

"We received some letters last evening—one from Emma, one from Don C. Smith, and one from Bishop Partridge— all breathing a kind and consoling spirit. . . . They were to our souls as the gentle air is refreshing. . . . But those who have not been enclosed in the walls of prison . . . can have but little idea how sweet the voice of a friend is; one token of friendship . . . awakens and calls into action every sympathetic feeling. . . it moves the mind backward and forward, from one thing to another, until finally all enmity, malice and hatred, and past differences, misunderstandings and mismanagements are slain victorious at the feet of hope; and when the heart is sufficiently contrite, then the voice of inspiration steals along and whispers, 'My son, peace be unto thy soul'" (*History of the Church* 3:293).

. . . all these things shall give thee experience, and shall be for thy good.

We often speak about the supportive role of women. The impact of Emma's letter on Joseph shows the very critical part she played and that all women can and do play. The support often comes before insight and revelation and is essential in its reception. Emma's comforting, consoling influence created for Joseph the atmosphere necessary for him to receive the Lord's inspiration, which enabled all of us to be edified by the magnificent truths of Liberty Jail.

Joseph emerged from Liberty in the spring of 1839 with a new-found strength and optimism conceived in the crucible of his imprisonment. "You will learn . . . " he said, "that walls and irons, doors and creaking hinges, and half-scared-to-death guards and jailors . . . are calculated in their very nature to make the soul of an honest man feel stronger than the powers of hell" (*History of the Church* 3:297).

He also obtained a deeper sense of charity for all men and a tolerance rare even in the most perfected men. These lessons he strived to teach the Saints. One of the last things he wrote from "this hell" was the following: "There is a love from God that should be exercised toward those of our faith, who walk uprightly, which is peculiar to itself, but it is without prejudice; it also gives scope to the mind, which enables us to conduct ourselves with greater liberality towards all that are not of our faith, than what they exercise towards one another. These principles approximate nearer to the mind of God, because it is like God, or Godlike" (*History of the Church* 3:304).

The door hinges still creak in Liberty. How grateful we may be that Joseph heard a more lovely music than their discordant sounds.

Mercy Fielding Thompson
on visiting Hyrum Smith in Liberty Jail

About the first of February 1839, by the request of her husband, my sister (Mary) was placed on a bed in a wagon and taken on a journey of about 40 miles to visit him [Hyrum Smith] in prison, her infant son Joseph F. then being about eleven weeks old. . . . The weather being extremely cold we suffered much on the journey.

We arrived at the prison in the evening. We were admitted and the doors closed upon us. A night never to be forgotten. A sleepless night. I nursed the darling babes and in the morning prepared to start for home with my afflicted sister, and as long as memory lasts will remain in my recollection the squeaking hinges of that door which closed upon the noblest men on earth. Who can imagine our feelings as we traveled homeward, but would I sell that honor bestowed upon me of being locked up in jail with such characters for gold? No! No! (Mercy Fielding Thompson, in Pearson H. Corbett, *Hyrum Smith, Patriarch* [Salt Lake City: Deseret Book, 1995], 201).

Spreading the Message

PROCLAIMING THE GOSPEL IN ENGLAND

ON SUNDAY, JUNE 4, 1837, JOSEPH SMITH DESCENDED from the Melchizedek pulpits in the Kirtland Temple and whispered to Heber C. Kimball, "Brother Heber, the Spirit of the Lord has whispered to me: 'Let my servant Heber go to England and proclaim my Gospel, and open the door of salvation to that nation'" (quoted in Whitney, 104). Thus was the expansive foreign missionary labor of the Church commenced.

There are few places on earth I enjoy visiting more than the British Isles. They gave to America so much in the way of literature, liberty, and scientific progress that it is pleasing to think America gave them back gifts equally precious. It is not the big cities of England that capture the heart, but the small villages and hamlets that dot the countryside. It was to

Maldon, Essex, England

Previous page: Eighteen-year-old Charles Penrose, the future editor of the Deseret News, *served a mission in this British village, where he wrote the well-loved hymn "O Ye Mountains High."*

Gadfield Elm Chapel

Opposite: This painting is of the Gadfield Elm Chapel in England, where the United Brethren met after secretly breaking away from the Church of England. Wilford Woodruff later baptized in a nearby pond hundreds associated with this group.

Herefordshire Beacon

Standing amidst the beautiful landscape of England, Brigham Young, Heber C. Kimball, and Willard Richards dedicated the land for proselyting and made the decision to print several thousand copies of the Book of Mormon.

Cobblestones

Opposite: This view of the twin English towns of Chatburn and Downham shows the area in which Elder Heber C. Kimball and his companion baptized so many in the Ribble River, which runs underneath the bridge shown in the background.

these tiny habitations that Heber C. Kimball and later Brigham Young and Wilford Woodruff preached the restored fullness; and it was to the poor, both in spirit and body, that their message sang.

Many of these places have changed little since the 1800s. To walk along the River Ribble in Preston, or to sit by the pond at Benbow's Farm, or to read of Heber's touching moments with the children in Chatburn, or to partake of the sacrament in the Gadfield Elm Chapel is to return in history and walk—not so much with the missionaries, but with our own ancestors, our own roots.

Their poverty and hardships touch the heart. Those who worked the lumber mills went blind from the sawdust, especially those who pulled the saw from below. "Top-notchers" working the log from above fared better. Lung disease was common in the textile industry and among glassblowers. In the "potteries" of Staffordshire lead oxide poisoned those who dipped ceramics in glaze. Tailors went blind sewing the red uniforms for the military in the dim light.

Life could be especially hard on children. Orphans were often rounded up in the big cities and sent to factories pulsing with the engines of the industrial revolution. Children went to work as young as six years of age. As one overseer in a Leicester mill related: "I have seen them [children] fall asleep, and they have been performing their work with their hands until they were asleep, after the billy had stopped, when their work was over. I have stopped and looked at them for two minutes, going through the motions of piecening (sic) fast asleep, when there was really no work to do, and when they were really doing nothing" (Robert Hughes, *The Fatal Shore* [New York: Alfred A. Knopf, 1987], 23).

My wife's ancestor, Ann Massey Clegg, who joined the Church in Lancashire, described her own poverty and anxious desire to immigrate to "the valley." Broken in health from her own labors, she watched her five-year-old son Thomas take his sisters' hands and walk into the cotton mill. There he would "work a twelve-hour day in a dingy, poor ventilated room breathing into his lungs the lint from the cotton." They subsisted on "a little weak tea with a bun or a little cake of oatmeal mush in the bottom of a teacup." When she first saw the Salt Lake Valley through Emigration Canyon, she whispered: "I am satisfied." She died a few weeks later, but her posterity would reap the blessings of her sacrifices.

Benbow Farm

This painting depicts the farm of John Benbow, one of the early founders of the United Brethren, a group that secretly separated from the Church of England. Many members of this group were later baptized into the LDS church by Wilford Woodruff.

The Amazon

Opposite: The title of this painting refers to the name of a ship that transported many members of the Church from England to the United States. It was this ship that Charles Dickens climbed aboard to observe the behavior of "the Mormons."

Wilford Woodruff
on preaching in England

When I arose to speak at Brother Benbow's house, a man entered the door and informed me that he was a constable, and had been sent by the rector of the parish with a warrant to arrest me. I asked him, "For what crime?" He said, "For preaching to the people." I told him that I, as well as the rector, had a license for preaching the gospel to the people, and that if he would take a chair I would wait upon him after meeting. He took my chair and sat beside me. For an hour and a quarter I preached the first principles of the everlasting gospel. The power of God rested upon me, the spirit filled the house, and the people were convinced. At the close of the meeting I opened the door for baptism, and seven offered themselves. Among the number were four preachers and the constable. The latter arose and said, "Mr. Woodruff, I would like to be baptized." I told him I would like to baptize him. I went down into the pool and baptized the seven. We then came together. I confirmed thirteen, administered the Sacrament, and we all rejoiced together.

The constable went to the rector and told him that if he wanted Mr. Woodruff taken for preaching the gospel, he must go himself and serve the writ; for he had heard him preach the only true gospel sermon he had ever listened to in his life. The rector did not know what to make of it, so he sent two clerks of the Church of England as spies, to attend our meeting, and find out what we did preach. They both were pricked in their hearts, received the word of the Lord gladly, and were baptized and confirmed members of the Church of Jesus Christ of Latter-day Saints. The rector became alarmed, and did not venture to send anybody else." (Matthias F. Cowley, *Wilford Woodruff: History of His Life and Labors* [Salt Lake City: Bookcraft, 1964], 118.)

It was not only the message of salvation that pulled the English Saints toward America and the long journey across ocean and prairie, but the hope of a better life among a caring people and the opportunity to bequeath to their children a more bounteous legacy.

To me, the ship docks in Liverpool are sacred ground. I cannot walk them without being overcome with the weight of tens of thousands of memories and deep emotions that occurred there. I walk along the Mersey River and hear returning down the tunnels of time the farewells, the tears, the joys, the fears of so many, many sacrificing Saints, some of whom would never see their final destination.

I myself slipped down the Mersey into the Irish Sea, hearing the wind in the sails pull the ship steadily away from the English coast, the words of my wife's great-grandfather resonating in my ears—a voice who spoke for thousands. His was a voice of irony, for the Liverpool Docks are a paradox of hope for the new and better life, but they are also tinged with longing for the old, familiar, deeply loved people and memories:

"I determined to leave home and country and go to Zion. I saved every penny to accomplish that object. . . . We left Liverpool on the 18th of May. Seeing my native land gradually sink into the horizon gave me a feeling of loneliness and uncertainty. I realized how dear it was; containing all that had given me a fullness of joy, mingled, sometimes, with a few sad moments. Loving parents had patiently nurtured and protected me all my twenty-one years. The companions of my childhood, all my relatives, some faithful friends, the land I revered, the ancient castles whose ruins I loved to explore, the stately mansions, splendid cathedrals, green lanes, cozy cottages, the hills and vales, green fields, and fragrant gardens ran through my mind. That I had left every human tie, even the creature of my thoughts, dreams, and prayers, whom I had loved from childhood, saddened me. My path was separating us by an ocean, a continent, perhaps, forever. And when the last speck of land faded from my wistful view, I asked the question: For what? For the conviction that the Church of Jesus Christ required it!" (*Life Story of Ernest Albert Law,* private journal in possession of family).

My path was separating us by an ocean . . . perhaps forever.

THE PACIFIC ISLANDS

THE SUCCESSFUL SPREADING OF THE GOSPEL in Europe was soon followed by calls to take the good news of the Restoration to the islands of the Pacific. As early as May of 1843, Joseph Smith called Addison Pratt on a mission to the Pacific Islands. The Doctrine and Covenants begins with an invitation for all the world to hear its glorious message. "Hearken ye people from afar; and ye that are upon the islands of the sea, listen together. For verily the voice of the Lord is unto all men . . . " (D&C 1:1). In a broader sense the phrase *islands of the sea* refers to all lands everywhere, but in a figurative and poetic sense it is the Lord's way of saying, "I am aware of even the tiniest stretch of land, and will bring all the blessings of my fulness to every place on earth." The message had already sounded on the island of England; those in the Pacific would soon follow.

I recall sitting on a flight to Hawaii next to a young man from Detroit who had never been out of the city before. He was on his way to a basketball camp and kept looking nervously out the plane window. Although we engaged in

Keaukaha Chapel
This two-story grass chapel near the airport at Hilo was the first LDS chapel built on the big island of Hawaii. In 1946 a tsunami hit the area, carrying away all of the white sand along the beach. All that remains now is the black lava rocks.

Addison Pratt
on the organization of the Tubuai Branch

I cannot express the heartfelt gratitude that came over me when I saw the tears of penitence trickle down their sea-worn faces, nor the warm emotions that vibrated my heart while, on their knees, I heard them thank their Father in Heaven that I had been casually thrown upon this island and had become the humble instrument in his hand in bringing them to see their lost condition. (R. Lanier Britsch, *Unto The Islands of the Sea: A History of the Latter-day Saints in the Pacific* [Salt Lake City: Deseret Book, 1986], 6–7.)

The Promise

In 1880, Joseph F. Smith promised the Hawaiian Saints that a temple would grace their land. This image reflects the fulfillment of his promise as it beautifully depicts a view of the Laie Temple from the sugar cane fields of Laie as it would have appeared in 1920—just one year after the temple had been dedicated by President Heber J. Grant.

pleasant conversation, I was aware that nothing I was saying to him alleviated his anxiety. Finally he asked me a question: "How do they find it out here with all this water?" How indeed?

We might ask a similar question of the Lord. Is there any place too small, or is there a people so remote that the message of salvation will not reach them? I believe the Lord took it very early to the "islands of the sea" so that we might understand that the gospel would come to all.

In truth, Addison Pratt decided to first preach the gospel on the island of Tubuai, 350 miles south of Tahiti. It is only three miles wide and six miles long. Here he enjoyed great success. From this tiny beginning, the Restoration spread throughout all of Polynesia. There is now a temple on every main island group in the Pacific. We must conclude that if God provided for His message to be known on a three-by-six-mile dot of land, He will surely see that it is preached in China and North Africa—and if there is a temple in Fiji and Tahiti, without doubt they will also rise in Shanghai and Calcutta.

Is there any place too small, or a people so remote, that the message of salvation will not reach them?

Nauvoo

STREETS OF THE CITY BEAUTIFUL

MY ANCESTOR EDWARD FARLEY was born in 1837 in Commerce, Illinois, so I have often wondered how the Farleys felt as the remnants of Governor Boggs's "extermination order" poured into his tiny settlement on the banks of the Mississippi and turned it into Nauvoo. Rather than sell out to the Mormons, the Farley family stayed on, and in time were baptized and became one with their guests.

Nauvoo Main Street

Previous page: I strived to capture the beauty of a place where the Spirit is so powerful and the sense of sacrifice is so palpable—and where the hand of the Lord in preserving its simplistic beauty is so strikingly obvious.

The Times and Seasons

In front of the Seventies Hall, which was created to be the meetingplace of the Quorum of the Seventy, stands The Times and Seasons *buggy. The publication came out twice a month and featured counsel from Church leaders, letters from missionaries, and revelations received by the Prophet.*

Lucy Mack Smith Home *This painting portrays the Lucy Mack Smith Home in Nauvoo, Illinois. With the Nauvoo Temple situated quietly in the background, this piece speaks peace and tranquility that must have prevailed during the happiest days in Nauvoo.*

What changes they saw over the next few years as canals were dug to drain the swamp and log homes were built, leading to those constructed of brick. In came the shops, the tradesmen, a newspaper, the social hall, the Masonic lodge, Joseph's Red Brick Store, schools, the Prophet's Mansion House, and the snug brick homes of Heber C. Kimball, Brigham Young, and Wilford Woodruff. In time he saw the beautiful temple built on the hill, dominating the bluffs that overlooked the river.

While Nauvoo was rising from the breeding grounds of malaria-ridden mosquitoes, other ancestors far away in the state of New York were accepting the gospel and preparing to respond to the magnetic pull of Nauvoo, the new center place for the gathering of the Saints. Harriet Austin Shaw left her family and headed for the "City of Joseph," her father riding behind her pleading with her not to join the Mormons. But she was fiercely determined and never looked back. The Farleys were from Virginia and the Shaws originated in Massachusetts, but Nauvoo was a melting pot of regions and nationalities. In time the Farley and Shaw families merged and bequeathed to their posterity all the blessings of the gospel. I have thanked and continue to express gratitude to them and to the Lord for their faith and sacrifices. Eight generations have descended from them. Did they realize when they chose to "throw in with the Saints" that they were choosing for thousands?

The Red Brick Store

Joseph Smith's Red Brick Store in Nauvoo was the location of Joseph's personal office, as well as the site where the Relief Society was organized and the first endowments were given.

Did they realize when they chose to "throw in with the Saints" that they were choosing for thousands?

George A. Smith wrote when visiting his ancestral home: "I have traveled to Egypt and the Holy Land, have seen the countries of Europe and met many of their most distinguished people, but I have encountered nothing that gives me more satisfaction than being here . . . on the ground where they [my ancestors] walked and lived and labored . . ." (George A. Smith, *Contributor* 4:3, Oct. 1882).

I share his sentiments. Coming to Nauvoo is a return to my roots—not only the broader heritage we all share in the lives of those early Saints and the men who led them, but the personal link that created all that is most dear, all that shaped my life. I have a perpetual sense of homesickness for the streets of Nauvoo, and every return is a turning back of time, a thinning of the veil, seeing Nauvoo through their eyes and becoming one with them.

I enjoy visiting the homes of the prophets with their ordered and intimate interiors, but it is in the shops and the open spaces that I feel most at home, for my ancestors would have walked these streets and done their business in these tiny spaces. Here they bought bread, here tin pails and lanterns, here candles, down the street barrels, medicine, rifles, or the latest edition of the *Times and Seasons*. I imagine they walked along the river in the cool evenings of summer; perhaps they fished, or swam. These were the parameters that defined the limits of their lives. And then there was Joseph, the soul of the city, the hub that held

Nauvoo Twilight

I often drive past our meetinghouse at dusk and see a few cars in the parking lot—and then I notice the light on in the bishop's office. I imagine it was much like this at dusk in Nauvoo: the First Presidency sitting around a simple wooden table in a home along one of its streets as the glow of lamplight filters through the windows. —————

Smith Noble Home

Above: Joseph and Mary Noble built this home in 1843. They remained there until 1846 when they fled west with the majority of the Saints. Before they left, they deeded the house to Lucy Mack Smith, who also planned to go west. However, she died in Illinois before she could fulfill this desire.

so many of its spokes together. They could hear him preaching in the open air and greeting the Saints on the streets, and with him Brigham and Heber and Hyrum and Willard.

As I do at all the Church history sites, I open the Doctrine and Covenants to ponder the refining words that have polished my life. The Lord told Joseph that Nauvoo was "a cornerstone of Zion, which shall be polished with the refinement which is after the similitude of a palace" (D&C 124:2). As for us all, the rough places must be smoothed by the sanding power of revealed truth. From the beginning it was the Lord's will that Nauvoo be visited in this manner, instructing Joseph to build "a good house, worthy of all acceptation, that the weary traveler may find health and safety while he *shall contemplate the word of the Lord;* and the corner-stone I have appointed for Zion" (D&C 124:23; emphasis added). In response to this the Nauvoo Inn was constructed and the Mansion House was used as a hotel. Later in the same revelation the Lord invited all visitors to Nauvoo, whether in the days of Joseph Smith or now, to *"contemplate the glory of Zion"* as displayed in Joseph's City (D&C 124:60; emphasis added).

Snow Ashby Home
Above: In the fall of 1843, the Ashby family moved to Nauvoo, where they shared a large duplex home with Elder Snow's family. The Ashbys, who had gained their wealth from being shipwrights and shoemakers, donated their wealth to help build the temple.

Sarah's Blossoms

While Wilford Woodruff was on his mission in England, his first daughter—a golden-haired two-year-old named Sarah—slipped from the bonds of mortality and was laid to rest in the Nauvoo Cemetery while the walls of the Woodruff home were only a few feet high. Imagine if you can the letter he received from his young wife, Phoebe. She did not complain about her wrenching loss or plead for him to return; instead, she wrote with wisdom and faith about a child too good for this earth—a child who had returned to the arms of her Savior. In this painting are the blossoms Sarah never saw in the backyard of a home in which Sarah never got to play . . .

The Prophet's Home Habits

Some of the home habits of the Prophet— such as building kitchen fires, carrying out ashes, carrying in wood and water, assisting in the care of the children, etc.—were not in accord with my idea of a great man's self-respect. . . . I reminded him of every phase of his greatness and called to his mind the multitude of tasks he performed that were too menial for such as he; to fetch and carry flour was too great a humiliation. "Too terrible a humiliation," I repeated, "for you who are the head, and you should not do it."

The Prophet listened quietly to all I had to say, then made his answer in these words: "If there be humiliation in a man's house, who but the head of that house should or could bear that humiliation?" Sister Crosby was a very hardworking woman, taking much more responsibility in her home than most women take. Thinking to give the Prophet some light on home management, I said to him, "Brother Joseph, my wife does much more hard work than does your wife."

Brother Joseph replied by telling me that if a man cannot learn in this life to appreciate a wife and do his duty by her, in properly taking care of her, he need not expect to be given one in the hereafter.

His words shut my mouth as tight as a clam. I took them as terrible reproof. After that I tried to do better by the good wife I had and tried to lighten her labors.

("Stories from the Notebook of Martha Cox, Grandmother of Fern Cox Anderson," Church Historian's Library, Salt Lake City, Utah; Lee C. LaFayette, "Recollections of Joseph Smith," Church Historian's Library, Salt Lake City, Utah.)

Visiting the Mansion House

Left: The Mansion House served as a social center for the Nauvoo Saints and Joseph Smith. It totaled twenty-two rooms, ensuring that there was always room for visitors. In this painting we see a visitor pulling up his carriage to the beautiful place of welcome.

Mansion House Roses _____

Below: The garden splendor in front of the Nauvoo Mansion House, which was used as a residence for the Prophet Joseph Smith and his family, as well as a hotel for important visitors to the area.

THE NAUVOO TEMPLE

Joseph's Nauvoo

Joseph and Hyrum crossed the river from Montrose to Nauvoo in a leaky dingy, using their boots to bail out the water. This dock area would have been where Joseph landed, and he would have walked up the street to his home, the Mansion House. Inside many of the houses were conspiring men and women who would eventually send him to Carthage, but his attitude of forgiveness was evident as he talked about his love for the good people who surrounded him. I portrayed the temple as being finished in this painting—Joseph had already seen it in vision, and this is how his spiritual eyes saw it.

PERHAPS MOST WORTHY OF CONTEMPLATION is the great work of the Nauvoo Temple, the crown of the Restoration. My footsteps always end on the hill overlooking the river where now the restored temple commands attention from every corner of the city. In this building my own ancestors first received the saving ordinances of eternity. It is appropriate that the temple ordinances for the living and the dead should dominate our thoughts as we visit Nauvoo. Joseph himself wrote while hiding from his enemies, "I now resume the subject of the baptism for the dead, *as that subject seems to occupy my mind, and press itself upon my feelings the strongest,* since I have been pursued by my enemies" (D&C 128:1; emphasis added).

If we will welcome the Lord's invitation and contemplate the glory of Zion, particularly as that glory relates to the temple, we can receive the joy Joseph Smith himself felt and put into some of the most eloquent words he ever penned. As his mind drifted back through the events of the past and the blessings of the temple, all which manifested so clearly the great goodness of God, he sang what could be called the hymn of the Restoration, the "new song" of praise. He invited all to sing with him—all mankind, all creation, all times.

Nauvoo the Beautiful
This painting portrays the peace and spiritual splendor of the Nauvoo era artfully blended with the present-day restoration of Joseph's temple. I painted this image to commemorate the 2002 Nauvoo Temple dedication.

"Now, what do we hear in the gospel which we have received? A voice of gladness! A voice of mercy from heaven; and a voice of truth out of the earth; glad tidings for the dead; a voice of gladness for the living and the dead; glad tidings of great joy. . . .

"Brethren, shall we not go on in so great a cause? Go forward and not backward. Courage, brethren; and on, on to the victory! Let your hearts rejoice, and be exceedingly glad. Let the earth break forth into singing. Let the dead speak forth anthems of eternal praise. . . .

"Let the mountains shout for joy, and all ye valleys cry aloud; and all ye seas and dry lands tell the wonders of your Eternal King! And ye rivers, and brooks, and rills, flow down with gladness. Let the woods and all the trees of the field praise the Lord; and ye solid rocks weep for joy! And let the sun, moon, and the morning stars sing together, and let all the sons of God shout for joy! And let the eternal creations declare his name forever and ever! And again I say, how glorious is the voice we hear from heaven, proclaiming in our ears, glory, and salvation, and honor, and immortality, and eternal life; kingdoms, principalities, and powers!" (D&C 128:19, 22–23).

The Nauvoo Temple was most noted in its architecture for the sun, moon, and star stones that so distinguished it. It is the dominant theme for it now, both inside and out, and many modern temples bear this imprint of Nauvoo. It was always a highlight of past visits to look into the carved face of the remaining sunstone and the more subtle features of the moonstones. I used to think the three sets of stones represented the three degrees of glory (which they may, as symbols can have many layers of meaning), but they seemed to be in the wrong position on the temple. Now, as I reflect, other thoughts come to mind.

In Revelation, John saw in vision a beautiful woman whom Joseph revealed represented the Church. She was "clothed with the sun, and the moon under her feet, and upon her head a crown of twelve stars" (Rev. 12:1). In three sections of the Doctrine and Covenants God said the Church would rise up and come forth "out of the wilderness of darkness" and shine forth "clear as the moon,

Wandle Mace on the Nauvoo Temple

The order of architecture was unlike anything in existence; it was purely original; being a representation of the Church, the Bride, the Lamb's wife. John the Revelator, in the 12th chapter, first verse, says, "And there appeared a great wonder in heaven; a woman clothed with the sun, and the moon under her feet, and upon her head a crown of twelve stars." This is portrayed in the beautifully cut stone of this grand temple.

(*Wandle Mace, Autobiography*, L. Tom Perry Special Collections Library, Brigham Young University, Provo, Utah, 207.)

Brigham Young on the first endowments in the Nauvoo Temple

MONDAY, [JANUARY] 12. —

One hundred and forty-three persons received their endowments in the Temple. I officiated at the altar. Such has been the anxiety manifested by the saints to receive the ordinances [of the Temple], and such the anxiety on our part to administer to them, that I have given myself up entirely to the work of the Lord in the Temple night and day, not taking more than four hours sleep, upon an average, per day, and going home but once a week.

Elder Heber C. Kimball and the others of the Twelve Apostles were in constant attendance but in consequence of close application some of them had to leave the Temple to rest and recruit their health.

TUESDAY, [FEBRUARY] 3. —

Notwithstanding that I had announced that we would not attend to the administration of the ordinances, the House of the Lord was thronged all day, the anxiety being so great to receive. . . . I also informed the brethren that I was going to get my wagons started and be off. I walked some distance from the Temple supposing the crowd would disperse, but on returning I found the house filled to overflowing.

Looking upon the multitude and knowing their anxiety, as they were thirsting and hungering for the word, we continued at work diligently in the House of the Lord.

Two hundred and ninety-five persons received ordinances.

(History of the Church 7:567, 579.)

and fair as the sun" (see D&C 5:14; 105:31; 109:73). The Church is a source of light for the world and that light has various qualities. It is a clarifying light that sheds truth upon every issue, problem, or situation. As the sun diminishes the darkness, so too will the fulness of the gospel chase away ignorance. It is a light as radiant, soft, and beautiful as moonlight. As John wrote: "For this is the love of God, that we keep his commandments: and his commandments are not grievous" (1 John 5:3). It is a guiding light sent forth by the Apostles, as constant as the stars. We can always get our bearing from these men.

The temple stones also mark our pathway back to God. If we were to "hie to Kolob," as the hymn invites (*Hymns*, No. 284), our pathway would leave the earth and pass first the moon, then the sun, then the stars in a higher and higher reach. As we stand by the temple, the stones encourage that upward journey and assure us that the doorway, the gate, the beginning of that road lies through temple doors.

Summer in Nauvoo

This painting portrays the Heber C. Kimball Home located in Nauvoo, with the Nauvoo Temple in the background and the Farr Home in the lower right. This image is a poignant reminder of the sacrifice, commitment, and industry of the early Saints.

A unique silence born of contrasts surrounds the jail.

MARTYRED AT CARTHAGE

THOUGH ALL SITES ALONG THE CHURCH HISTORY TRAIL HAVE THE SPIRIT, some invite an intensity of feeling and reflection. No one comes away from Carthage Jail without an appreciation for the price that was paid by Joseph and Hyrum that we might adequately value their greatest legacy—that of words. John Taylor indicated three times in his account of the martyrdom that they died "to seal the testimony of this book [the Doctrine and Covenants] and the Book of Mormon" (D&C 135:1; see also verses 3 and 6). Our greatest act of empathy with their sacrifice will ever be to search and to live by the words recorded in those two books. As John Taylor so eloquently stated it, "the reader in every nation will be reminded that the Book of Mormon, and this book of Doctrine and Covenants of the church, cost the best blood of the nineteenth century to bring them forth for the salvation of a ruined world" (D&C 135:6).

Carthage Jail

This painting depicts the site of the martyrdom of the Prophet Joseph Smith on June 27, 1844. It is unique in that it portrays Carthage from the perspective of the jailer's children as they returned home that night after fleeing from the mob that killed the prophet.

Willard Richards to Joseph Smith

Joseph said to Dr. Richards, "If we go into the cell, will you go in with us?"

The doctor answered, "Brother Joseph, you did not ask me to cross the river with you—you did not ask me to come to Carthage—you did not ask me to come to jail with you—and do you think I would forsake you now? But I tell you what I will do; if you are condemned to be hung for treason, I will be hung in your stead, and you shall go free."

Joseph said, "You cannot."

The doctor replied, "I will."

(History of the Church 6:616.)

View from Montrose

Montrose is situated across the Mississippi River from Nauvoo and is the site where Joseph and Hyrum Smith escaped a mob in June of 1844. Emma sent word that a posse had come for them that morning, warning that the governor had promised to place troops in Nauvoo until the brothers submitted to arrest. From Montrose, Joseph and Hyrum returned and made their journey to Carthage Jail to surrender.

There is a unique quiet that surrounds the jail. I hear it every time I arrive. It is a silence born of contrasts created on that sultry June day in 1844. If we listen, the sounds of that day return as a memory embedded in our collective consciousness—the nervous conversations of the four men—the hopeful sadness of John Taylor's voice singing, "A poor wayfaring man of grief hath often crossed me on my way . . . "—the brief pause of hesitant awareness when every tiny sound is perceived—the increasing noises of mob fury beginning in the distance, then closing in on the jail—the pounding of feet climbing the stairs—the gunshots—Hyrum's plaintive cry, "I am a dead man!"—Joseph's pleading, "O Lord my God!"—the final shouts and fading fearful voices—then silence, profound, universal, heaven-reaching silence, punctuated only by the cleansing patter of summer rain. It all comes back to us, so familiar, so present, so final, so constantly tragic, so hauntingly personal. Yet, behind it all, Joseph's serene assurance, "I am calm as a summer's morning; I have a conscience void of offense towards God, and towards all men" (D&C 135:1, 4). He taught us how to live. He showed us how to die.

Return to Nauvoo

I tried to capture in this painting the city of Nauvoo as Joseph and Hyrum would have seen it, returning to face the charges that ultimately led to their martyrdom. Certainly Joseph knew that his death was shortly at hand; I can't imagine the anguish that filled his heart as he saw his beautiful city for what he knew was one of the last times. Pivotal to this perspective is the temple—an edifice that provided for the Saints the ordinances essential to exaltation.

Westward Migration

The Journey *Previous page: As I traveled through Missouri, I found a child's grave on an isolated stretch of trail. I saw in my mind's eye a father, finished with the business of wrapping and burying his child, working now to hitch the horses and resume his journey. I saw, too, the broken-hearted mother, not wanting to leave, torn with the anguish of abandoning the little body in the wilderness. I wanted to capture on canvas their raw grief—but I also wanted to capture their determination to move forward, the hallmark of faith and resolve that characterized the Saints on the journey.*

Webb Blacksmith Shop *This Nauvoo winter scene includes the Webb Blacksmith Shop and the Seventies Hall (background) as they would have appeared in 1844.*

THE PIONEER TRAIL

I UNDERGO A KIND OF TRADITIONAL RITUAL every time I leave Nauvoo. It is a walk from the blacksmith shop down the "trail of tears" to the Mississippi River. I walk slowly, looking frequently behind me to the lovely city and the temple reigning above it, and letting the land speak. Under Brigham Young's leadership there were two areas of feverish activity in those last months and weeks of Nauvoo—the completion of the temple and preparations for the journey west. The Lord had told them to "build a house unto me" with the added caveat that "if you do not these things at the end of the appointment ye shall be rejected as a church, with your dead . . . " (D&C 124:31–32). The lessons of Missouri were not forgotten; the temple would be completed in spite of mob fury or the Saints' limited resources. There were difficult and trying times ahead, and the Saints would need the power the full temple covenants could give them. So between the temple and the blacksmith shops and wheelwrights, the energies of a motivated people were divided. Even while construction moved ahead on the temple, the coming departure was signaled by the sounds of hammers pounding metal on anvils and the hissing release of heat as ox shoes and wheel rims were plunged into cold water.

Nauvoo Inn *After the Saints left Nauvoo, Louis Bidamon—who became Emma Smith's second husband—vowed to finish building the Nauvoo Inn for her. I wanted to capture in this work the difference between the Saints and those who followed. The part of the Inn constructed by the Saints is exquisite in both beauty and workmanship, much like that of the temple. Beginning with the gables, it is easy to see that the subsequent construction was done not only with leftover scraps, but was constructed by a builder who exercised much less care.* ——————————————————

What fears and regrets, hopes and anticipations trailed down the road to the river in wagon after wagon? A chorus of emotion still echoes through the dust and around the once-abandoned buildings. There was no "Come, Come, Ye Saints" to cheer and strengthen in those early months. My own ancestors crossed the river into the sea of mud that marked the prairies in springtime Iowa. Frost was a mixed blessing, for it hardened the ground for the oxen and prevented the iron rims of the wagon wheels from cutting deeper into the earth. But February turned into March, and mud was the demon of the day.

I have a journal account of the day-by-day progress across the plains written by Angelina Farley, one of my ancestors. Her entries tersely record what was on the minds of so many as they struggled across the plains of Iowa to Winter Quarters and then across Nebraska and Wyoming, through the gentle rising slope of the South Pass cut in the Rocky Mountains, and on to the final descent into the Salt Lake Valley:

June 23rd. *A little child died with the measles this evening in the wagon next behind us.*

June 27th. *Passed five fresh graves yesterday after crossing a creek. . . . The men were frightened at the report of cholera ahead and left several graves by the road of those who had died with the cholera. Some Mormons.*

June 28th. *Rained this morning. Cold and uncomfortable. Several quite unwell in our camp. Passed the fifteenth new-made grave.*

July 3rd. *We were the last ten. A child died and was buried yesterday. Another this morning, making six persons out of our camp; four children, two men. We have passed 33 graves besides.*

July 7th. *Passed four graves, among them was that of Brother Adamson's babe.*

July 9th. *Asa quite sick. Hard wind and some rain last night. Passed six graves.*

The entries continue on with a daunting regularity. July 10—six graves; July 12—six graves; July 13—five graves; July 15—twelve graves; July 16—fourteen graves; July 17—five graves; July 19—thirteen graves; July 20—nine graves; July 21—nine graves; July 22—eleven graves; July 23—ten graves; July 28—twelve graves; July 30—fifteen graves. Yet, when discouraged and weakened, as the family approached Ft. Laramie on July 31, Angelina wrote:

Mother Farley talks hard of staying at Ft. Laramie, a movement that seems to me almost death, if not quite. I cannot bring my mind to submit. I started with the expectation of entering the Valley before I stopped and now to fall short of it. . . . I might as well be laid under the sod of these plains almost. Passed fifteen graves today.

Winter Quarters

Winter Quarters was a tribute to the efficiency of the LDS people. Those arriving immediately had a place to stay—often in a tent or the back of a wagon—and some built log cabins for their families until they were ready to head out on the trail. Men and women worked in the fields, gathered their provisions, and tried to secure enough money to make the journey. Brigham Young noted in his journal that he often fell asleep to the ringing of axes as determined men worked through the night.

While at Winter Quarters, on the 17 of February, 1847, President Young had a very interesting dream which he related to the brethren. He dreamed that he went to see Joseph, the Prophet, and when he met him he looked perfectly natural. . . . President Young said . . . "If you have a word of counsel for me I shall be glad to receive it."

Joseph stepped towards him, looked very earnestly yet pleasantly, and said, "Tell the brethren to be humble and faithful and be sure to keep the Spirit of the Lord, and it will lead them aright. Be careful and not turn away the small, still voice; it will teach them what to do and where to go; it will yield the fruits of the kingdom. Tell the brethren to keep their heart open to conviction, so that when the Holy Ghost comes to them their hearts will be ready to receive it. They can tell the Spirit of the Lord from all other spirits—it will whisper peace and joy to their souls; it will take malice, hatred, strife and all evil from their hearts, and their whole desire will be to do good, bring forth righteousness and build up the kingdom of God. Tell the brethren if they will follow the Spirit of the Lord, they will go right."

(*Millennial Star*, Sept. 23, 1873, 597–98.)

They passed the landmarks that are so familiar to us, but not to them, for the great westward migrations of the 1800s were just beginning. The Platte, the Sweetwater, the Green, Chimney Rock, Independence Rock, the Devil's Gate, South Pass, Big Mountain—the names continue on and on as long and tiring as the plodding march of oxen and the singing creak of the wheels. Still, the tiny mounds of soil or piles of rocks weighed on their minds more forcefully than mountain ranges or river fords.

THE HANDCART COMPANIES

Trial of Hope— Captain Willie

This painting depicts Captain Willie and Joseph Elder of the Willie Handcart Company during the moment they finally found the rescue party sent from Salt Lake to aid the handcart pioneers.

IN THE LONG YEARS OF MORMON WESTERN MIGRATION, one year—1856—stands out as potently as the "days of 47." The poor of Europe—the "Brits" and the "Danes," infused with a longing for Zion—would come pulling their handcarts. But schedules and plans do not always flow with the smooth workings of inspiration and common sense. Late departures, green wood, hastily constructed carts, short provisions, ill health, neglected counsel, over-active zeal, and an early winter would produce the greatest tale of suffering in the decades of the Mormon trail. Caught in the snows and chill of an early winter, the Willie and the Martin companies endured the sufferings that have been memorialized year after year by modern "pioneers" in bonnets and felt hats.

Three times I have pulled a commemorative handcart through the places of deepest suffering—Martin's Cove, Sixth Crossing of the Sweetwater, Rocky Ridge, Rock Creek Campground—and each time the oft-repeated stories are overwhelming. Why did the Lord not bump the jet stream a hundred miles to the north and let the blizzards and the cold stalk the empty mountains and plains of northern Wyoming? Was He not moved by the agonies of those who

Trial of Hope—One Last Hill

This image depicts a member of the Willie handcart company as she scans the horizon looking for the last hill. In this painting you see the fortitude, conviction, and determination she exercised as well as the cold, fatigue, and loneliness she endured.

Sacrifice gives weight to testimony and pulls it deep into the heart.

left all for Zion, many of whom could not even speak the language of the land into whose interior they entered?

Did He see the thousands of youth and families that year by year would come to remember, my own children part of them? He who sees all time as the present, did He hear my own prayers for those children that faith would sink deep in their hearts, that the sacrifices of those who came before would somehow sanctify their own growing testimonies? Sacrifice gives weight to testimony and pulls it deep into the heart. Without sacrifice there is no depth of faith, and in the Spirit's celestial economy the sacrifices of previous generations can anchor the faith of succeeding ones. The tragedies played out on the high plains of Wyoming surely gave weight to the testimonies of the Restoration for all of us.

Rock Creek always demands long silent moments at the grave site of the Willie Company victims who perished from exhaustion and cold. When I sleep at Rock Creek my mind drifts back to one of them, Bodil Mortensen of Denmark, whose parents had sent her ahead to the Valley with relatives. Surely they were praying back in Denmark for her safe arrival—surely with equal, if not greater, anxiety than that with which I pray for my own little ones. But Bodil died of exhaustion and frost just short of her final destination and safety. She had been sent out to gather firewood, but while returning she rested next to a handcart wheel, went to sleep, and died before she was discovered. She was only nine years old. Who has the wisdom to sort out such paradoxes of destiny? All I can do is thank her and those who suffered with her for the legacy of faith, courage, and compassion she left for the children of today

Jens and Elsie Nielsen
Willie Handcart Company

The end appeared to be near and certain for Jens. His feet became so frozen he could not walk another step. . . . At this point Jens said to Elsie, "Leave me by the trail in the snow to die, and you go ahead and try to keep up with the company and save your life." If you believe men have a monopoly on strength and courage, then pay heed to Elsie's immortal words when she said, "Ride, I can't leave you, I can pull the cart." Jens had to suffer the humiliation of riding while Elsie pulled like an ox. He later said when describing this ordeal, "No person can describe it, nor could it be comprehended or understood by any human living in this life, but those who were called to pass through it."

(Stewart E. Glazier and Robert S. Clark, eds., *Journal of the Trail* [Salt Lake City: The Church of Jesus Christ of Latter-day Saints, 1997], 166.)

John Chislett
on seeing the Rescue Party's approach

On the evening of the third day after Captain Willie's departure, just as the sun was sinking beautifully behind the distant hills, on an eminence immediately west of our camp several covered wagons, each drawn by four horses, were seen coming towards us. The news ran through the camp like wildfire, and all who were able to leave their beds turned out en masse to see them. A few minutes brought them sufficiently near to reveal our faithful captain slightly in advance of the train. Shouts of joy rent the air; strong men wept till tears ran freely down their furrowed and sun-burnt cheeks and little children partook of the joy which some of them hardly understood, and fairly danced around with gladness.

(John Chislett Journal)

The Valley

A view of the Salt Lake Valley from the top of Little Cottonwood Canyon.

and for all of us who feel the weight of our own testimonies pulled deeper by their sacrifices.

I sat at the top of the sand dune that sweeps into Martin's Cove years ago with a close friend whose own ancestor huddled against the wind in that sheltered place of pain. He too was moved beyond expression with the accounts of suffering, but the Lord granted him, and me through him, the blessing of eternal perspective. "As I sat here," he began, "I saw through the Spirit's eye a young girl about eleven or twelve, coming toward me. I was weeping, but she said, 'Don't mourn for us! Our suffering was not equal to the hundredth part of what we have received.'"

Does it answer all the questions or atone for decisions that, perhaps, should not have been made—for suffering God could not have willed, yet allowed? Possibly? We are all in the hands of Providence, and our strength must be born by the knowledge that that Power is good, that that Being is love itself, and that when all is weighed in the balance, nothing will have been endured in vain.

COLONIZING THE MOUNTAIN WEST

Mount Olympus and the Pugh Home

Previous page: When Mrs. Pugh, who lived in this house, was a little girl, it was her job to get the meat from the butcher. Whenever he rang the bell on his wagon, neighbors would come outside and place their order— and he would cut up the meat for them. The butcher was my grandfather, Charlie Fagg, then a young man in his early twenties! I later used the Pugh Home as my gallery—a tribute to both my grandfather, who made his living there, and to Mrs. Pugh, who inspired my imagination with her stories.

Logan Temple Spring

This painting depicts the beautiful Logan Utah Temple amidst the natural springtime beauty of Cache Valley.

FOR MANY, THE MILES WALKED ALONG THE MORMON TRAIL were not the last they would take. Salt Lake was the destination on each pioneer's lips, but Brother Brigham's vision included a colonization that would spread the Saints across the entire Utah Territory and beyond. Every water source flowing out of the mountains, every spring, every natural resource was explored, plotted, staked out, and inhabited. So they packed up again, traveling up and down the Wasatch Front, into "Dixie," Cache Valley, the Iron Mission, the Basin. In time the "stakes" of the great tent of Zion would be driven from Cardston, Alberta, at the Canadian border to Mesa in the hot deserts of Arizona.

They accepted these "mission calls" with the same stoic patience and fortitude that had sustained them from New York to Jackson, from Kirtland to Winter Quarters. Calls to leave the Valley were not done in the private offices of

Millcreek Mill

Mt. Olympus stands majestic in the background of this rendering of one of twelve mills built along East Millcreek (southeast of Salt Lake City). This view is from the original site of the John Neff Mill, built at 2700 South & Evergreen Ave.

Rose Canyon

This painting highlights the late-afternoon splendor of the Rose Canyon area, located in the Oquirrh Mountains west of Herriman, Utah.

General Authorities, but from the pulpit or in casual conversations between friends on the street. Robert Gardner, called as one of the cotton missionaries to St. George, heard his name had been placed on a list as a "volunteer." He left his sawmill and met George A. Smith at Church headquarters, who validated the rumor. "I looked and spat," Gardner wrote, "took off my hat, scratched my head, thought and said, 'All right.'" He still had to present the move to his family. "We go where we are told to go, and make a track, and

we have always been glad to do so" (Nels Anderson, *Desert Saints* [Chicago: University of Chicago Press, 1942], 232).

Then when the young finished their parlor courting, they traveled back to the heartland temples, journeying along the honeymoon trail into St. George, or down from the north into Logan or Salt Lake City.

I recall the excitement I felt as a child when June came, school was over, and my mother, my sisters, and I packed the car for our trip to Utah. There was no air conditioning, so we hung a canvas

Calls to leave the Valley were not done in private offices, but from the pulpit or in casual conversations on the street.

water bag from the front of the car and left Southern California in the darkness of night. We stopped for gas in Las Vegas—sometimes still hotter than a hundred degrees at two or three in the morning. As the dawn broke, we strained our eyes for the Utah-Nevada border sign, then St. George and the bright white of the temple, stark against the red rocks. We were in Mormon country. The highway ran through every tiny Mormon settlement from St. George to Ogden, our final destination. The landscape changed from the flat deserts of Nevada to cedar-covered hills, orchards, irrigated hay fields, fences, cattle, tiny islands of shade trees framed by the spine of the Wasatch Mountains. Cedar City, Parowan, Beaver, Fillmore, Scipio, Nephi, Payson, Provo—we scratched through the names on the map. Then Salt Lake Valley and the contest of who could first see the Salt Lake Temple—then the tallest building in the city. Bountiful, Centerville, Farmington, finally Ogden, and we reached the end of our journey. I was then off to the ranch and a summer of work in a boy's paradise.

My uncle was a rancher, bred from pioneer stock. He was as old as the West, and I have never known a better man. He instilled in

Sweet Peas

The Reading Family Home is located in Centerville, Utah. The Readings ran a family business growing vivaciously colored sweet peas.

me a love for the "old times," before television and air conditioning, before the freeways bypassed the fruit stands that marked every hamlet of Brigham Young's "Deseret." He taught me how to shoot a stream of milk into a kitten's mouth, curl a grasshopper on a hook and lay it in the ripples above a deep hole where the "rainbows" waited, cut a calf out of the herd and hold him down for the branding, catch a horse in the open field with a willow halter, hitch a team to the rake and lay the hay into windrows, and square up a hay stack with that most useful of tools—a pitchfork. I learned the sweet ache of muscles that have worked hard all day in the summer sun; the fresh rinse of river water poured over head and back and arms; the quick, deep falling to sleep in the bunkhouse at sunset; and the chill, shivering feel of the air at four in the morning when it would all begin again.

My aunt ruled the kitchen, which was the center of the house, and the smells that filled that room—well, it makes me smile to think about it. I'd stand next to the wood-burning stove in an aura of heat and breathe in. Fried chicken rolled in batter, hot buttered scones dripping with homemade currant jam, oatmeal mush at five in the morning buried under a layer of maple syrup or half an inch of molasses, apple pies steeped in cinnamon cooling on the front porch, warm bread cut two fingers thick, cornbread light and easy with honey, buckwheat hot cakes, venison from the canyon, trout from the river, eggs from the henhouse, buttered corn on the cob so hot it burned your fingers, bread pudding drowned in morning milk, dumplings moist from the boiler, mashed potatoes pooled with beef gravy. They knew how to eat in those days, and I pity the fast-food generation.

St. George Temple

To me, the St. George Temple is one of the most stunning examples of what a people are willing to sacrifice for their God. I tried to imagine what it would have been like for travelers from California to come through an absolutely desolate section of the country and then, as they came up over the Bloomington rise, to see that beautiful temple against those red hills. I included the irrigation ditch because for those Saints, the water was their temporal lifeblood, just as the temple was their spiritual sustenance.

Under the direction of Brigham Young, the St. George temple was built in under six years, making it the first temple completed in Utah after the arrival of the Mormon pioneers, and was dedicated April 6, 1877.

Surrounding the canal are the mulberry trees the pioneers planted to provide sustenance for the silkworms they raised. Saints from the Midwest and New England had experience in producing silk, and a few had brought mulberry seeds with them, since silkworms eat mulberry leaves around the clock the first forty days after they hatch. In 1855, Brigham Young imported additional mulberry seedlings and silkworm eggs from France; he then began a campaign to get Utah women into the silk business in an effort to help the Saints become financially self-sufficient from the sale of the silk. Silkworm eggs were introduced to Washington County in 1871. Despite support from the Relief Society and organization of the Deseret Silk Association, this social and economic experiment failed because of the rigors and exacting conditions required to raise the silkworms.

Manti Temple

Right: I love the story behind this painting, because it demonstrates that the best things are often found in the most unexpected places. My daughter Quinn—three or four at the time— and I had spent the entire day traipsing and driving around Manti, looking for the perfect perspective of the temple. I sketched quite a bit. I took a lot of pictures. But I simply didn't find what I wanted. Finally it got dark, and with a slight sense of defeat, Quinn and I got on the highway and headed for home. Suddenly, I looked in the rear-view mirror, and there it was! Framed by the edges of the mirror was the perfect view of the temple. I pulled off to the side of the road, jumped out of the car, and starting snapping pictures. As a result, I've always called this my "rear-view mirror painting."

Isaac Chase Home

Below: Located in modern-day Liberty Park, this painting shows the Isaac Chase Home and farm that still stand today. Isaac Chase offered a prayer at the Salt Lake Tabernacle that the Saints' farms be saved from the crickets destroying them. It was then that the seagulls arrived, devouring the crickets and saving the crops. This home was later deeded to Brigham Young.

I spent every summer until I was sixteen at the ranch, and if anything ever happened that wasn't basis for a warm memory, I have forgotten it. I remember the lantern's glow at twilight, the constant steady rush of the river accompanied by the crickets and cicadas, Saturday night baths in the galvanized tub on the porch, stained fingers from picking berries with only half going into the pail, hawks circling in the warm currents of the canyon, watermelon cooling in the river, rain from a sudden thunderstorm rattling on a tin roof with the booming thunder in the distance. We lived close to creation and were neighbors with the beavers and the badgers, the packrats and the mule deer, and the mountain lions. Lizards sunned in lazy, silent solitude on the hot rocks and chuckers clucked in the sagebrush.

I know how to turn the ringer on the phone the right number of times to reach every ranch in the valley. I know the best time of the night to lie out under the sky and count shooting stars or watch a full moon's pale light cast shadows down the canyon walls. I know the dark hiding places for "kick the can," how to walk the flume without falling, where to find arrowheads and how to strip the bark from a willow, notch it, and slide it back to make a whistle. I know the welcome fright of ghost stories and how to tell them, too. All the simple, sweet, stately joys once felt and seen and known by the old-timers were mine to experience.

And every 24th of July on Pioneer Day, my aunt would have us sing in robust enthusiasm,

> "They the builders of the nation. . . .
> They unfurled the flag of truth,
> Pillar, guide, and inspiration
> To the hosts of waiting youth.
> Honor, praise, and veneration
> To the founders we revere!
> List our song of adoration,
> Blessed honored Pioneer"
> (*Hymns*, No. 36).

Israel Barlow Home 1894

This painting portrays the historic Israel Barlow home that still stands in Bountiful, Utah today. Born in 1806 and baptized in 1832, Israel Barlow was a member of Zion's Camp, served as a missionary in England, and was an original member of the Quorum of the Seventy. His quiet, steadfast, and unwavering service to the Lord throughout his lifetime is a wonderful example of so many of the early Latter-day Saint pioneers.

View from Main

Above: A view of the Salt Lake Valley in 1888, five years before the completion of the Salt Lake Temple.

Eagle Gate Trolley

Right: This painting celebrates a wonderful dichotomy: the Saints took great care to preserve their past while eagerly looking forward and embracing new technology. Salt Lake City boasted some of the first underground power lines and an advanced trolley system that took riders throughout much of the Salt Lake Valley. At the same time, great care was taken to preserve the Beehive House—an adobe structure—and to replace the Eagle Gate many times throughout the years, maintaining both as treasured landmarks.